THE WORLD NEEDS MORE CANADA

OUR GREATEST ATHLETES

Maggie Mooney with the
CANADIAN SPORT ADVISORY COUNCIL

THE WORLD NEEDS
MORE CANADA

GREYSTONE BOOKS
D&M PUBLISHERS INC.
Vancouver/Toronto

Greystone Books
An imprint of D&M Publishers Inc.
2323 Quebec Street, Suite 201
Vancouver BC Canada V5T 4S7
www.greystonebooks.com

Cataloguing data available from Library and Archives Canada
ISBN 978-1-55365-606-7

Editing by Michelle Benjamin
Text design by Heather Pringle and Jessica Sullivan
Jacket design by Indigo Books and Music Inc.
Jacket photograph by (left to right):
Chantal Petitclerc: The Canadian Press/Eugene Hoshiko
Gordie Howe: Harold Barkley
Adam van Koeverden: COC/The Canadian Press/Andre Forget
Clara Hughes: Vancouver Sun/Ian Lindsay
Jimmy McLarnin: Canada's Sports Hall of Fame
Barbara Ann Scott: Canada's Sports Hall of Fame
Ferguson Jenkins: The Canadian Press
Nancy Greene: Canada's Sports Hall of Fame/Michael Burns Collection
Maurice Richard: Harold Barkley
Mike Weir: The Canadian Press/Matt York
Interior photograph credits on page 133
Printed and bound in Canada by Friesens
Printed on acid-free, FSC-certified eco-paper

We gratefully acknowledge the financial support of the Canada Council for the Arts,
the British Columbia Arts Council, the Province of British Columbia through the Book
Publishing Tax Credit, and the Government of Canada through the Canada Book Fund
for our publishing activities.

Mixed Sources
Cert no. SW-COC-001271
© 1996 FSC
FSC

CONTENTS

INTRODUCTION

THE IDEA IS deceptively simple: produce a book that celebrates the 100 greatest Canadian athletes of all time. My first clue that this would be more challenging than I had originally thought came during a dinner party with family and friends. I mentioned the book and ignited a fervent debate. By the end of the evening I had a list of athletes—some I'd never heard of, many we hadn't thought of including, all worthy of consideration for our final list. This enthusiastic discussion was repeated whenever the topic came up. Canadians, it became clear—even those who don't follow sports that closely—are passionate about their athletes.

The selection process generated a new level of debate. We assembled the Canadian Sport Advisory Council by asking several well-known sports journalists from across the country to send their top Canadian athletes ranked from 1 to 100. Each expert produced a carefully considered list, including renowned stars and household names, as well as many athletes whose stories have been forgotten. The deliberations became more complex as we suddenly had a file of more than 400 outstanding athletes.

Now what?

We developed a point system and mathematical formula that combined the lists and tallied the results in a fair and reasonable way, and created a freshly ranked list of 100 athletes. We sent this new group to the panel and let the discussions begin. Opinions were expressed—many contradictory, all well informed and passionate—and arguments for inclusion or banishment were voiced. Further changes were made as athletes moved up or down in the ranking, and in and out of the top 10, the top 20, the top 50. Eventually we had a satisfying and defensible list of the 100 greatest Canadian athletes of all time.

Several challenging questions arose during this selection process. The first was key to the whole project: What constitutes "greatest"? The term is subjective—the 400-plus names submitted by one small group of sportswriters proves how varied the definition can be. Yet certain signs tell us when we are in the company of the great. For example, an accumulation of awards and prizes point to notable accomplishments—it won't surprise anyone that most of the athletes on this list are recipients of Canada's highest annual athletic honours.

Olympic and World Championship medals and records are also reliable markers of greatness. For team athletes, greatness shows up in All-Star picks, national team selection, and in honours for specific positions—best defensive player, best pitcher, best quarterback—as well as most-valuable-player honours. For retired athletes, great achievement is acknowledged by induction in Canada's Sports Hall of Fame and individual sports' halls of fame, as well as prestigious membership in the Order of Canada.

The next key question was, who counts as Canadian? Only those born in Canada? Only Canadian citizens? What about the Americans who played their entire football careers in the CFL? We decided to include athletes who were born in Canada, those who had immigrated to Canada at a young age—we are a nation of immigrants, after all—and those who came to represent Canada internationally, clearly embracing "Canadian" as part of their identity.

We had further deliberations. Some thought we had too many hockey players; others said we had too few, or the wrong ones, or in the wrong order. Given the prominent place that hockey holds in the Canadian psyche, it's not surprising that just over a quarter of the athletes on the list play hockey. The image of a child learning to skate on the backyard pond appeared repeatedly in the athletes' childhood stories, and most of the boys—and many of the girls—regardless of the sport they excelled in, wanted at some point to be a professional hockey player.

The next challenge was rating athletes from different eras. Can you fairly compare players from the pre-expansion NHL with the post-expansion era—Rocket Richard versus Wayne Gretzky? And what about training techniques, equipment, and medical intervention? Here the "what ifs" arise. What if Bobby Orr could have undergone modern knee surgery? What if the progressive training methods of marathoner Tom Longboat had been recognized rather than criticized? What if skier Anne Heggtveit could have used fibreglass rather than wooden skis, and quick-release bindings?

The most passionate debates concerned two very different athletes: Terry Fox and Ben Johnson. Compelling arguments were launched in favour of including or excluding each from the list. In the end, we decided that Fox resides in a category all his own—he didn't win a gold medal or break world records, and he wasn't competing against other athletes, yet he performed an astonishing athletic feat, and his achievement shines brightly in the eyes of Canadians. Some say this decision is driven by emotion, not logic, and they might be right.

As for Johnson, the argument went something like this: He was undeniably a phenomenal athlete who was simply unlucky—he was the one to get caught using banned substances, when it is known that many of his competitors were also using performance-enhancing drugs. And if that's true, is it fair to exclude Johnson? We decided that it was. He has been banned for life by the International Olympic Committee, his world record has been expunged from the books, his Olympic gold medal was rescinded, and—fair or not—he is no longer recognized as a world champion. Ben Johnson does not appear on the list.

So the task was impossibly thorny yet fascinating. Comparing apples and bananas, hockey with slalom skiing, swimming with curling, marathon runners with race car drivers, female athletes with male athletes. The arguments continue (at least at my family table), and while no final consensus was reached among the writers—they offered sturdy reasoning for their choices based on years of experience covering Canada's finest sports stars—there was general acceptance of the process and of the final list.

GREATNESS OFTEN goes hand in hand with legacy. Many of these athletes had a profound influence on their sport, not only while they competed, but also in their post-athletic lives. Some have gone on to impressive careers in sports management, business, and politics, and their legacies have been great and far-reaching. Some have been deeply involved in worthy charitable or social change initiatives such as Right to Play; some have launched their own foundations—George Chuvalo, for example, and Steve Nash. While this ranking and these biographies focus exclusively on each athlete's competitive career, those achievements outside of the sports arena are no less significant and that legacy no less important.

A particular type of heroism emerges in the stories of some of these athletes. While many seem blessed with long and productive careers or only minor hurts, others battle with chronic or career-altering injuries—Mario Lemieux, Harry Jerome, and Silken Laumann come to mind. Although these athletes are not ranked higher because of these struggles, their courage is noteworthy.

Several of the athletes on the list are still actively competing, and so their lists of awards and achievements are still growing. While I was writing this book, Martin Brodeur matched and then broke Terry Sawchuk's NHL record for most regular-season shutouts. New athletes were inducted into Canada's Sports Hall of Fame. Medals were won, records were set, new levels of achievement were reached. And new athletes emerge into our consciousness every day. Fresh superstars are in training, waiting for the opportunity to claim their place on future editions of this list.

Interestingly, and not by design, winter and summer sports are represented almost equally. It's a tribute to the tenacious spirit of this snowy nation with its short summers that we have managed to produce so many top-level athletes who excel in summer sports such as rowing, baseball, cycling, golf, and track.

For Canadian sports lovers, this book is an opportunity to learn about the achievements of your favourite athletes and to be introduced to stars from a different era or a less-familiar sport. These top athletes come from myriad backgrounds—rural and urban, wealthy and poor, immigrant and home-grown, east and west and points in between—yet all share a common drive for excellence, a willingness to push themselves to the top of their chosen sport. We proudly showcase this athletic drive in these pages and celebrate the breadth of competitive sports in Canada.

This book is a celebration of the commitment and accomplishments, not only of these great athletes, but also of every Canadian—child or adult—who ties on skates or running shoes, straps on skis or climbs into a canoe, or bounces a ball on the hardwood for hours on end.

Play on!

HONOURS

· James Norris Trophy–1977, 1980
· Conn Smythe Trophy–1978
· Hockey Hall of Fame–1995
· Canada's Sports Hall of Fame–2004
· Number 19 retired by Montreal Canadiens

100 Larry Robinson

1951 (Marvelville, Ontario)– **LARRY ROBINSON—ONE OF** hockey's greatest defensive players—led the Montreal Canadiens to 6 Stanley Cups, including 4 in a row from 1976 to 1979.

Robinson played junior hockey with the Brockville Braves and the Kitchener Rangers and turned professional with the Nova Scotia Voyageurs of the American Hockey League, helping them win the Calder Cup in 1972.

Drafted by the Canadiens in 1971, Robinson hoisted his first Stanley Cup in 1973— his rookie year. He played 17 seasons with the Habs and 3 more with the L.A. Kings, appearing in 227 playoff games over an astounding 20 consecutive playoff seasons— an NHL record.

Robinson towered over his opponents, and his formidable size and chaotic blond curls landed him his friendly nickname "Big Bird," but he was respected as one of the hardest hitters in the game.

Robinson played for Team Canada during their 3 Canada Cup victories in 1976, 1981, and 1984. This 10-time All-Star retired in 1992 and still holds the best career plus-minus record (+730) in NHL history. In 2000, Robinson added his name to the Stanley Cup for a 7th time, this time as coach of the New Jersey Devils.

99 Jacques Villeneuve

1971 (Saint-Jean-sur-Richelieu, Quebec)– JACQUES VILLENEUVE SPENT much of his childhood on wheels, in a motorhome, following his famous father's Formula One (F-1) racing circuit. Gilles Villeneuve's tragic death in 1982 didn't deter Jacques from racing. After a successful run driving karts as a teenager, and later racing on the F-3 and F-4 circuits, Villeneuve claimed the F-1 title that had eluded his father.

In 1995 Villeneuve was the youngest driver and the only Canadian to win the Indianapolis 500. A year later he joined the F-1, placing second in his first race and second in the season, launching a frenzy of excitement that Canadian auto-racing fans hadn't known since the elder Villeneuve's glory days.

Villeneuve clinched the F-1 title the next season with 7 wins. Like his father, Villeneuve thrived on high-risk racing and pushed himself to the limits of speed and technology. He survived spectacular collisions and thrilled fans with his bad-boy persona.

Villeneuve moved to the newly formed British American Racing team in 1999, but returned to F-1 with Team Renault in 2005. Since 2006, he has raced the LeMans sports car circuit, and with NASCAR, Speedcar, and Top Race v6, amid rumours of a return to F-1.

98 Charmaine Hooper

1968 (Georgetown, Guyana)–
SOCCER STAR CHARMAINE Hooper excelled in international play with 130 games—or "caps"—and 71 goals. But that only begins to describe her achievements on the soccer pitch.

Hooper, raised in Ottawa, was an original member of Canada's national team in 1986. She was a dominating force throughout her career with the Women's United Soccer Association and Women's Premier Soccer League, and internationally with clubs in Norway, Italy, and Japan. She twice led the Japanese L-League in scoring, and in 1997 was league MVP. A year later she topped the USL W-League in scoring and again was crowned MVP.

A dangerous striker with a reputation for aggressive play, Hooper led North Carolina State University to the ACC championship in 1988, setting school records for goals and points.

Hooper was twice named Canadian Player of the Year. She played in the Women's World Cup in 1995, 1999, and 2003, the Gold Cup in 2000 and 2002, and in 1999 she was game MVP in the FIFA Women's World All-Stars special match against the United States.

HONOURS
· Canadian Player of the Year–1994, 1995
· FIFA Women's World All-Stars MVP–1999

HONOURS

· CanWest Media Female
Athlete of the Year–2007

97 Jennifer Heil

1983 (Edmonton, Alberta)–
COMMITTED, WISE, AND extremely skilled, Canada's freestyle skiing star Jennifer Heil knew from an early age that she would be a high-level athlete, and she took well-considered risks to get there.

In her first Olympics, at Salt Lake City in 2002, 19-year-old Heil missed the podium with a 4th-place finish in moguls. She then made the precarious decision to take a year off. Heil had no intention of quitting but she understood that she would never reach Olympic gold unless she dealt with the extreme pain caused by racing the gruelling moguls course. Working with an outstanding team of trainers, Heil transformed her approach to fitness. The risk paid off.

The next year Heil was World Cup mogul champion. She clinched the World Cup title from 2004 to 2007, and at the 2006 Olympics in Turin, Heil reached gold—the first-ever Olympic moguls medal for Canada. A knee injury kept her out of competition in 2008, but she returned stronger than ever, winning multiple World Cup gold and silver in 2009–10. Heil skied brilliantly to another Olympic medal—a silver—at the 2010 Vancouver Games. This 8-time national champion has earned more than 45 World Cup medals—a number that is sure to increase as her remarkable career continues.

HONOURS

· Hec Gervais Playoff MVP
Award–1997, 2009
· World Curling Tour's Men's
MVP–2009

96 Kevin Martin

1966 (Killam, Alberta)–
KEVIN MARTIN IS one of the most rock-solid curlers on the planet, with record successes in national and international competitions.

Martin won the Canadian Junior Championship in 1985 and a silver medal at the World Juniors one year later. In 1991 he won his first Brier—the Canadian Championship—and at the Worlds that year again scored silver and a pass to the 1992 Albertville Olympics, where curling was a demonstration sport.

Martin skipped his team to the Brier again in 1992, 1995, 1996, and in 1997, when they won the title. In 2002, Martin made his second Olympic appearance, this time capturing the silver medal.

Martin, known as "The Old Bear," is renowned for pulling off near-impossible shots in complex situations. Other curlers use the expression "to do a Martin" when they attempt extremely difficult throws.

In 2006, Martin re-formed his team with an eye to the 2010 Olympics. In the lead-up to the Games, Martin's crew was on fire, winning the 2008 Brier and World Championship, and in 2009 Martin won his 4th Brier, his 3rd Canada Cup title, and came second in the World Championship.

At the 2010 Vancouver Games, Martin skipped his team through the round robin without losing a single game—the first Olympic curling team to do so. In the final match against Norway, Martin threw the hammer to capture Olympic gold in front of a jubilant crowd singing "O Canada."

95 Susan Nattrass

1950 (Medicine Hat, Alberta)–
FOR LONGEVITY ALONE, Susan Nattrass's career is extraordinary. The champion trapshooter successfully lobbied for the inclusion of women's shooting events in the Olympic Games and competed at a world-class level for 40 years, including in 6 Olympics.

Nattrass' father, also an Olympian, taught her to shoot as soon as she could hold a gun. She performed outstandingly at her first major competition—the 1968 Golden West Grand competition in Nevada. Angry at being written off as just a "young Canadian girl," 18-year-old Nattras triumphed against 1,200 other competitors, mostly men.

Through the '70s and early '80s, Nattras led the world in women's trapshooting—she held the National Women's Trapshooting title for 15 years, was the top woman trapshooter in North America for 5 consecutive years, and won 6 world championships between 1974 and 1980, including a world record 195 of 200 targets in 1978.

Nattrass was the first woman shooter in Olympic competition at Montreal in 1976, and in 1990 she was the first woman to compete in the shotgun event at the Commonwealth Games. She captured 2 bronze medals at the 2002 Commonwealth Games, Pan American bronze in 2003, and 3 more Commonwealth medals—2 silvers and a bronze—in 2006. Nattrass competed in her 6th Olympics in Beijing in 2008 almost 40 years after her first international competition.

94 Mark Tewksbury

1968 (Calgary, Alberta)-
RECORD-BREAKER MARK TEWKSBURY honed his razor-sharp backstroke as a young swimmer at the University of Calgary. He ranked 4th in his first international competition at age 17 and a year later captured 2 gold medals at the 1986 Commonwealth Games—in 100-metre backstroke and 4×100-metre medley relay.

At the 1987 Pan-Pacific Games, Tewksbury won 2 silvers and a gold, raising expectations for the upcoming Olympics in Seoul. But the competition was tough, and he came home with a disappointing 5th-place standing and a relay silver.

Undaunted, Tewksbury set his sights on the next Olympics, becoming one of the top backstrokers of all time along the way—silver and bronze at the 1989 Pan-Pacifics, double gold at the 1990 Commonwealth Games, 2 silvers each from the 1991 Worlds and Pan-Pacifics, and a handful of world records.

Tewksbury was prepared when he entered the pool in Barcelona at the 1992 Summer Olympics. He captured 100-metre backstroke gold in a dramatic, come-from-behind, .06-second victory—an Olympic-record performance. He and his teammates also won bronze in the 4×100-metre relay. The Canadian swimming hero received 3 athlete-of-the-year honours that year.

Tewskbury retired in 1992 with 21 national championship titles—11 individual and 10 relay.

HONOURS

· Swimming Canada's Male Swimmer
  of the Year–1987, 1991, 1992, 1993
· Lou Marsh Trophy–1992
· Lionel Conacher Award–1992
· Norton H. Crow Award–1992
· Canadian Olympic Hall of Fame–1993
· Canada's Sports Hall Of Fame–1995
· International Swimming Hall of Fame–2000

93 Mike Bossy

1957 (Montreal, Quebec)–
DESPITE HIS RELATIVELY short, 10-year NHL career, marksman Mike Bossy scored 573 goals in just 752 games—a goals-per-game average higher than any player in NHL history. Bossy—"Mr. Fifty"—also notched more consecutive 50-plus goal seasons (9) than any other player and shares the most 60-plus seasons mark (5) with the Great One, Wayne Gretzky.

Bossy—a quick-release master with a deadly shot—was revered for his uncanny positioning and his ability to beat goaltenders. In Juniors with the Laval Nationale, Bossy scored a phenomenal 309 goals in 4 seasons. In his 1977–78 rookie year with the New York Islanders, 20-year-old Bossy won the Calder Trophy with a record-breaking 53 goals.

During the Islanders dynasty in the early 1980s, Bossy's powerful shot was key to 4 straight Stanley Cup wins, including the 1983 sweep over Gretzky and the Edmonton Oilers. During the 1981–82 season, Maurice Richard was on hand to congratulate Bossy when he became the first to match Richard's 1945 record of 50 goals in 50 games.

The powerful right-winger and 8-time All-Star—known also for his clean play and sportsmanship—suffered from a chronic back injury from years of being on the receiving end of fierce cross-checking. He had to cut short his dynamic career, retiring in 1987.

HONOURS

· Calder Trophy–1978
· Conn Smythe Trophy–1982
· Lady Byng Trophy–1983, 1984, 1986
· Hockey Hall of Fame–1991
· Canada's Sports Hall of Fame–2007
· Number 22 retired by the New York Islanders

92 Anne Heggtveit

1939 (Ottawa, Ontario)-
THE 2010 VANCOUVER Olympics marked the 50th anniversary of Anne Heggtveit's remarkable slalom performance that captured Canada's first Olympic skiing gold medal and launched Canada as a world-class skiing force.

Born into a champion skiing family, Heggtveit strapped on her first skis at age 2. She won her first race at 7 and by 9 had been invited to join the Canadian Ski Team. At only 15, Heggtveit surprised the world by becoming the youngest ever to win the challenging Holmenkollen Giant Slalom in Norway. A year later she suffered a broken leg in a training accident; the next seasons were fraught with injury, but by 1959 she

was back in winning form. She finished that season as the first North American to win the most prestigious event in alpine skiing—the Arlberg-Kandahar.

Heggtveit captured 2 Alpine World Champion gold medals in 1960—in Slalom and Combined Alpine—becoming the first non-European to win a World Championship Alpine skiing title.

At the Squaw Valley Olympics in 1960, Heggtveit flew through the technically difficult slalom course to claim gold—Canada's first. She finished a remarkable 3.3 seconds ahead of her competitors, still the largest margin for any winner in Women's Olympic or World Cup slalom history. She retired following those Games.

HONOURS

· Calder Trophy–1980

· James Norris Trophy–1987, 1988, 1990, 1991, 1994

· Lester Patrick Trophy–2003

· Hockey Hall of Fame–2004

· Number 77 retired by Colorado Avalanche
  and Boston Bruins

91 Raymond Bourque

1960 (Saint-Laurent, Quebec)– RAY BOURQUE WAS Boston's number-1 draft pick in 1979 and his impact was immediate—the 18-year-old tallied 65 points, more than any other rookie defenceman in NHL history at the time, and secured the Calder Trophy.

Bourque ruled the ice with his offensive prowess and defensive excellence. In 1983–84, he hit a career-high 31 goals and 96 points. In 21 years with the Bruins, Bourque led the team in scoring 5 times, and in 1997–98 he became only the 5th NHLer to notch 1,000 assists. Appointed captain in 1988, Bourque led the Bruins to 2 Stanley Cup finals.

Despite his spectacular career in Boston, Bourque had yet to win a Stanley Cup, so in 2000 he requested a trade. With the Colorado Avalanche he continued to make his mark, including a record 19th consecutive All-Star appearance. In his first—and last—full season in Colorado, Bourque reached his ultimate goal, finally capturing the Stanley Cup.

Bourque retired in 2001 with impressive stats: all-time Bruins leader in points (1,579), assists (1,169), and games played (1,612), and first in the league in all-time points and goals (410) by a defenceman. He represented Canada in 3 Canada Cup tournaments (1981, 1984, 1987), and at the Nagano Olympics in 1998.

HONOURS

· Calder Trophy–1974

· James Norris Trophy–1976, 1978, 1979

· Hockey Hall of Fame–2001

· Number 5 retired by New York Islanders

90 Denis Potvin

1953 (Hull, Quebec)–
HARD-HITTING, FEARLESS DEFENCEMAN
Denis Potvin led the New York Islanders through their glory years of the 1980s. During his 8-year reign as captain, the Islanders won 4 consecutive Stanley Cups (1980–83) and never failed to reach the playoffs.

Potvin, a star junior player in Ottawa, was the NHL's first overall draft pick in 1973. The struggling expansion Islanders placed great hope in Potvin, and he delivered, winning rookie-of-the-year honours and—with his physical defensive style and strong offensive abilities—revealed his potential to become one of the game's greatest all-round players.

The 3-time Norris Trophy winner's skills included a lightning-fast wrist shot, finesse passing, and one of the deadliest hip checks of all time, making him one of hockey's premier backliners. Potvin described his love for the rough, physical game: "The most fun I had was hitting. I enjoyed the contact, and hockey provided me with a lot of opportunities."

In his 15 years with the Islanders, Potvin broke most of Bobby Orr's records (he played 403 more games than Orr) and was the first defenceman to reach 1,000 career points. When he retired in 1988, Potvin's record of 310 goals and 742 assists (1,052 points) was the league's all-time record for a defenceman.

89 Henri Richard

1936 (Montreal, Quebec)–
HENRI RICHARD IS often compared to his well-known older brother, Maurice, but the "Pocket Rocket" was an NHL standout in his own right. In fact he notched more points, played more games, and won more Stanley Cups than his heroic sibling. A revered all-round playmaker, he's still the only individual whose name is engraved on the Cup a remarkable 11 times as a player.

Richard joined the Montreal Canadiens in 1956 after a stellar junior career, just in time to contribute to 5 straight Stanley Cup victories. In his 3rd year he led the league in assists and was selected to the First All-Star Team.

Through the late 1960s the Habs' Cup run continued and Richard was key, netting the overtime winner to clinch the series against Detroit in 1966. In the 1970s the now-veteran continued to make significant plays, scoring the tying and winning goals in the final game of the 1971 Cup series against Chicago. In 1973—wearing the honoured "C"—Richard passed the magic 1,000-point milestone, only the 9th player in league history to reach that mark. He contributed to one more Stanley Cup victory, his 11th.

Richard retired in 1975, having won Stanley Cups in more than half of his NHL seasons.

88 Daniel Igali

1974 (Eniwari, Nigeria)– DANIEL IGALI'S VICTORY somersault and exuberant kiss of the Canadian flag after his gold-medal victory at the 2000 Sydney Olympics is unforgettable. Igali explained, "That gush of exhilaration and appreciation for this country just came naturally. For me, being a Canadian is about being free, being a world citizen; it's a land of dreams where you can achieve whatever you want."

Igali was born in one of the poorest villages in Nigeria in 1974, and he learned to wrestle gambolling with his 20 siblings. His natural talent earned him a national title at age 16, and he reached African champion status in 1993 and 1994. After the 1994 Commonwealth Games in Victoria, the 20-year-old team captain chose to remain in Canada as a refugee, hoping to pursue an education and escape from the civil war at home.

Igali attended Simon Fraser University, and after 2 years of dedicated training he joined the school wrestling team in 1997, winning an astounding 116 consecutive matches over 2 years. At the World Championships in 1999, Igali won gold and set his sights on the Olympics.

At the Sydney Games, Igali was unbeatable, winning every competition including the final gold-medal match—Canada's first-ever Olympic gold in wrestling.

Igali retired after the 2004 Athens Olympics.

87 Sylvanus "Syl" Apps

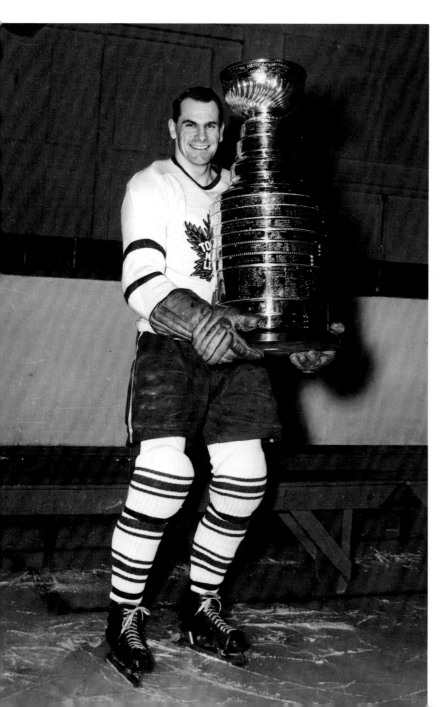

1915 (Paris, Ontario)–1998

IN AN ERA of bamboo poles and hard landings, Syl Apps was a champion pole-vaulter. He won a gold medal at the 1934 British Empire Games and competed for Canada in the 1936 Berlin Olympics.

Multi-talented Apps was also star halfback and captain of the McMaster University football team. Conn Smythe was so impressed by Apps's abilities that he convinced him to switch to hockey and signed him to the Toronto Maple Leafs in 1936. A year later he earned the first-ever Calder Trophy.

Except for two years during World War II, Apps played centre for the Leafs from 1936 to 1948. An offensive powerhouse and playmaker, he captained Toronto to 3 Stanley Cups including the legendary 1942 comeback series against Detroit. After losing the first 3 games, the Leafs came back to win the Cup—the only time in NHL history this has been accomplished.

Known for his abstinence (no drinking, smoking, or swearing) and on-ice manners, nice-guy Apps won the Lady Byng Trophy in 1942 after an entire penalty-free season.

Apps' granddaughter Gillian Apps plays on the Canadian Women's Hockey Team.

HONOURS

· Eddie James Trophy–1951, 1955, 1956
· CFL Outstanding Canadian Player Award–
  1955, 1956
· Lionel Conacher Trophy–1955
· CFL Hall of Fame–1969
· Canada's Sports Hall of Fame–1975
· Member of the Order of Canada–1998
· Number 95 retired by Edmonton Eskimos

86 Norman "Normie" Kwong

1929 (Calgary, Alberta)-
NORMIE KWONG—THE FIRST Chinese-Canadian player in the CFL and holder of over 30 records—was one of the greatest running backs in league history and, at the time, the youngest player to win a Grey Cup.

Nicknamed the "China Clipper," Kwong played his entire professional career in his native province of Alberta. Kwong joined the Calgary Stampeders in 1948 and was instrumental in the only "perfect season" in CFL history—undefeated in regular season and playoffs.

Kwong was traded in 1951 to the Edmonton Eskimos, where he played for 10 seasons. The pint-sized fullback was a solid blocker and brilliant faker. He scored 93 touchdowns and rushed for a total of 9,022 yards—an outstanding record that doesn't include the 2 years he played before statistics were kept.

Kwong led the Eskimos to 3 consecutive Grey Cups. Three-time leading rusher in the Western Division, 5-time All-Canadian Fullback, and the CFL's top Canadian player in 1955 and 1956, Kwong was also Canada's top male athlete of 1955. After retiring, he became part owner of the Calgary Flames, joining the elite few whose name is on both the Grey Cup and the Stanley Cup. In 2005 Kwong was appointed Lieutenant-Governor of Alberta.

15

HONOURS

· Hockey Canada Female Hockey Breakthrough
  Award–2005
· Black Hockey and Sports Hall of Fame–2007
· International Ice Hockey Hall of Fame–2008

· Canada's Sports Hall of Fame–2009
· Angela James Bowl is awarded to Canadian
  Women's Hockey League's top scorer

85 Angela James

1964 (Toronto, Ontario)-
ANGELA JAMES—THE FIRST female superstar in the modern game—is often called
the Wayne Gretzky of women's hockey. But
James's start was quite different from the
Great One's. As a young skater in the early
'70s, James had to overcome the countless
limitations on girl's hockey: a lack of teams,
scarce ice time, and often outright hostil-
ity towards a girl who dared to play hockey.
Her talent and passion for the game drove
James to persevere. She sharpened her
skills, becoming a top-notch power forward
with explosive speed, finely honed offensive
and defensive abilities, and a wicked shot.

In the early 1980s James was a stellar player at Seneca College as well as the
dominant player in the Central Ontario
Women's Hockey League—she was league
MVP 6 times. She played for Team Canada
at the first 4 Women's World Championships—1990, 1992, 1994, and 1997—leading
Canada to 4 golds and notching 22 goals
and 34 points in 20 games. At the National
Women's level, James won more than 12
medals and was named MVP 8 times.

James was in the first group of 3 women
inducted into the International Ice Hockey
Hall of Fame in 2008.

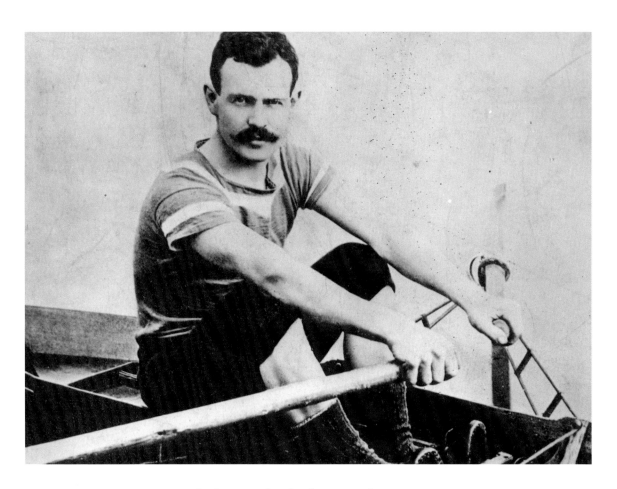

84 Ned Hanlan

1855 (Toronto, Ontario)–1908

IN AN ERA when rowing was one of the most popular spectator sports, champion oarsman Ned Hanlan drew the largest crowds and the biggest betting purses.

As a boy Hanlan lived on Toronto Island and developed his rowing skills during his daily commute to school across Toronto Bay. Hanlan won the Ontario Championship in 1875 and—encouraged by "Hanlan's Team," a group of wealthy Torontonians eager to bet on him—he turned professional the following year. Hanlan pioneered the use of the sliding seat and rotating oars, which gave the slightly built rower an advantage over his larger opponents.

Thousands came to watch the world's greatest rower as much for his entertaining style as for his skill. Hanlan often toyed with his opponents—the wily rower would sprint out fast then slow down if his opponent was too far behind. On one occasion Hanlan turned his boat around, rowed back to his opponent, then raced him to the finish line.

In 1880, at his first World Championship in England, Hanlan's reputation preceded him—the banks of the Thames were overrun by 100,000 spectators. Hanlan captured the crown that day, becoming the first individual world champion in Canadian history. He successfully defended his world title 6 times.

HONOURS

· Canada's Sports Hall of Fame–1955

HONOURS

- Art Ross Trophy–1976, 1977, 1978
- Lester B. Pearson Award–1976, 1977, 1978
- Hart Trophy–1977, 1978
- Conn Smythe Trophy–1977
- Lionel Conacher Award–1977
- Lou Marsh Trophy–1977
- Officer of the Order of Canada–1980
- Hockey Hall of Fame–1988
- Canada's Sports Hall of Fame–1996
- Number 10 retired by Montreal Canadiens

83 Guy Lafleur

1951 (Thurso, Quebec)- GUY LAFLEUR FULFILLED his childhood dream—playing for the Montreal Canadiens. He joined the storied team in 1971 after a stellar record-setting junior career. He scored 29 goals in his first NHL season and two years later, "The Flower" soared to his first of six 50-plus-goal/100-plus-point seasons. Three-time NHL scoring leader, Lafleur contributed to 5 Stanley Cup victories, including 4 in a row from 1976 to 1979.

Lafleur's on-ice performance slowed down, and unwilling to be less than great, he retired in 1984 as the Canadiens all-time leader in points and assists (1,246/728)— a record that still stands—and holder of the second-highest goal total behind Rocket Richard (518). Lafleur reached the magic 1,000-point mark in only 720 games, the fastest ever at the time, and still holds the franchise record for points-per-game (1.3) and points in a season (136).

In 1988 Lafleur returned to the NHL for 3 more seasons, 1 with the New York Rangers and a final 2 at home in Quebec with the Nordiques. In those final 3 years, beloved Lafleur—6-time All-Star and fan favourite for his spectacular rushes, awesome slapshot, and flying blond hair—received a standing ovation every time he played at the Montreal Forum.

82 Tony Gabriel

1948 (Burlington, Ontario)- TONY GABRIEL—ONE OF the most dependable and hardworking players in Canadian football—owned the tight end position and changed the look of the game. Amazingly, he missed only 2 games in his 11-year career, and set a record by catching passes in every single game he played for 8 seasons.

Gabriel played college ball at the University of Syracuse in New York, where he set records for receiving. The New York Giants pursued him, but Gabriel was eager to return to Canada. He started for the Hamilton Tiger-Cats in 1971 and led them to Grey Cup victory in 1972.

In 1975 he joined the Ottawa Rough Riders. In his most memorable CFL moment, Gabriel snagged the winning touchdown pass in the end zone in the final seconds of the 1976 Grey Cup game.

Gabriel led the East Division in receiving 4 seasons in a row (1975–78), and in 1978 he won the CFL's Most Outstanding Player Award (the last Canadian to receive the honour). In 11 seasons, he caught 614 passes for 9,832 yards and 69 touchdowns, and was 3rd in the league and first among all-time Canadian receivers.

HONOURS

· Outstanding Canadian Player, CFL East Division–1974
· Lew Hayman Trophy–1976, 1977, 1978, 1981
· Dick Suderman Award–1976
· Jeff Russel Trophy–1978
· CFL Outstanding Player Award–1978
· CFL Outstanding Canadian Player Award–1974, 1976, 1977, 1978
· Canadian Football Hall of Fame–1985
· Canada's Sports Hall of Fame–1985

HONOURS

· Inaugural Lou Marsh Trophy–1936
· CP Male Athlete of the Year–1936
· Canadian Olympic Hall of Fame–1950
· Canada's Sports Hall of Fame–1997
· The Phil A. Edwards Memorial Trophy is presented
  annually to Canada's outstanding track athlete

81 Phil Edwards

1907 (Georgetown, British Guiana [now Guyana])–1971

NICKNAMED "MAN OF BRONZE" in recognition of his 5 Olympic bronze medals, runner Phil Edwards was the inaugural winner of the Lou Marsh Trophy. He set 13 Canadian track records, and was Canada's most-decorated Olympian for 66 years.

Edwards moved to Canada as a young man with hopes of advancing his running career. He was invited to compete for Canada in the 1928 Amsterdam Olympics as a member the infamous track team that included Percy Williams and Bobbie Rosenfeld. Edwards finished 4th in the 800 metres and won his first bronze with the men's 4×400 relay team.

While studying at McGill University's medical school, Edwards captained the school's track team. He led the squad to 6 intercollegiate titles and competed in several international track and field competitions including 2 more Olympics.

At the 1932 Los Angeles Olympics, Edwards won 3 more bronze medals—in the 800 metres, 1,500 metres, and the men's 4×400 relay. Four years later, at the infamous 1936 Berlin Olympics, Edwards, like American Jesse Owens, was one of several black athletes who competed and triumphed in front of Adolf Hitler. Edwards captured a bronze medal in the 800-metre event— a Canadian 5-medal record not broken until Cindy Klassen won her 6th in 2008.

80 James "Jimmy" McLarnin

1907 (County Down, Ireland)–2004
BOXING LEGEND JIMMY McLarnin was one
of the best welterweight fighters of all time.
Over his 14-year professional career, this
2-time world welterweight titlist beat 13
world champions and won 63 of his 77 professional fights.

McLarnin immigrated with his family to
Canada at age 3 and developed his fighting
skills as a spunky boy defending his newspaper corner in downtown Vancouver. He
turned professional at 15 and, after a dozen
successful fights in Canada, looked to the
U.S. The young fighter, nicknamed "Baby-
Faced Assassin," lost his first title match

against lightweight champion Sammy
Mandell. Over the next 5 years McLarnin
defeated Mandell twice, along with a string
of other top boxers.

In 1933 McLarnin won his first title
bout against welterweight champion Young
Corbett III in a first-round knockout. He
lost the title to Barney Ross in 1934 in 3
epic 15-round fights in New York. Ross won
the first bout; 4 months later McLarnin
regained his crown, then lost the final fight
in a narrow points decision.

McLarnin retired in 1936 at only 29.
Sixty years later, *Ring Magazine* called him
the 5th-greatest welterweight of all time.

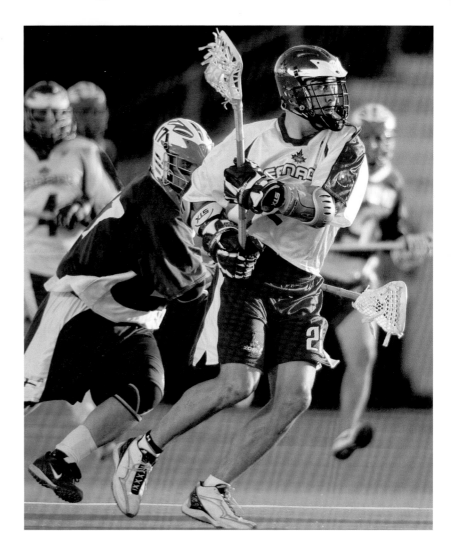

79 Gary Gait

1967 (Victoria, British Columbia)-
GARY GAIT IS considered to be the premiere
lacrosse player of all time—the Wayne
Gretzky of his sport. Renowned for his
exhilarating plays, the star mid-fielder
broke all National Lacrosse League scoring
records, led teams to a string of championships, and even invented lacrosse's version
of a slam dunk.

Gait launched his professional career in
1991, winning NLL rookie of the year. His
15 career records include all-time leading
scorer (1,091 points), most goals (596), most
goals in a season (61), most points in a game
(14), and 6-time league MVP.

Gait played for Canada from 1990 to
2006. At the 2006 World Championship
Gait wrapped up his international career
with 4 goals in the 4th quarter to lead Canada to an historic victory over the United
States.

Together with his identical twin brother,
Paul—also an outstanding player—Gait
expanded the popularity of lacrosse in North
America. Gait will also be remembered
for his signature move—the "Air Gait"—in
which he leapt acrobatically over the crease
from behind the 1.8-metre net, and—air-
borne—stuffed the ball into the goal.

Gait came out of retirement in 2009 to
play the inaugural season with the Toronto
Nationals of Major League Lacrosse.

78 Edward "Eddie" Shore

1902 (Fort Qu'Appelle, Saskatchewan)–1985
EDDIE SHORE—ONE OF hockey's original
tough guys—was revered for his scoring
touch and end-to-end rushes, and feared for
his bone-crushing body checks.

Shore joined the Regina Caps of the
Western Canada Hockey League in 1925,
and skated for the (hockey-playing) Edmonton Eskimos the next year. In Edmonton he
found his natural place on defence and was
tagged the "Edmonton Express."

The WCHL folded in 1926, and the Boston Bruins of the newly formed NHL picked
up Shore. His aggressive style and impressive puck handling made a big hit in Bean-
town, and in his first season he notched 130
penalty minutes while also scoring 12 goals.
He solidified his gritty reputation the next
year by sitting out a record 165 minutes.
Two years later Shore's determined play
and dominating style helped to carry the
Bruins to their first Stanley Cup. Shore won
the Hart Trophy 4 times—a record for a
defenceman. In 1939—Shore's final full season in Boston—the Bruins won their second
Stanley Cup.

The next year Shore purchased his own
team, the Springfield Indians of the AHL,
becoming an owner-player while also still
playing in select games for the Bruins (and
later the NHL's New York Americans).

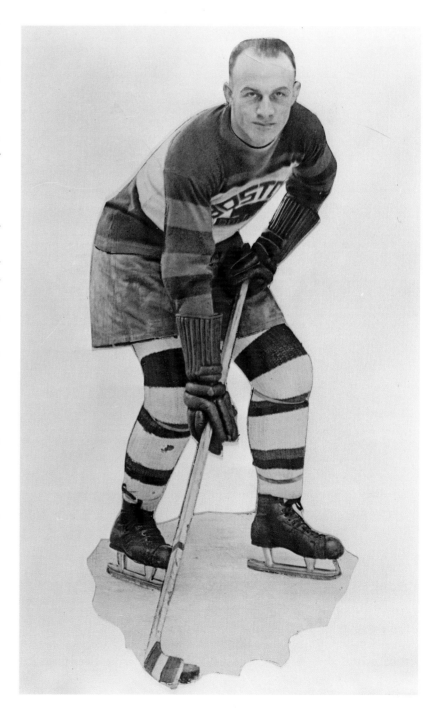

HONOURS

· Wilson and McCall Trophy–2001, 2002
· Lou Marsh Trophy–2001
· Skate Canada Hall of Fame–2008
· Canadian Olympic Hall of Fame–2009

77 Jamie Salé & David Pelletier

1977 (Calgary, Alberta)–
1974 (Sayabec, Quebec)–

JAMIE SALÉ AND DAVID PELLETIER, Canadian figure skating's most charismatic duo, were on a winning streak heading into the 2002 Olympics in Salt Lake City. The reigning world champions had 9 consecutive titles and hoped this momentum would lead to the first non-Russian pairs gold medal since the 1960 Olympics.

But it wasn't to be. Oh, wait... Yes, it was.

Salé and Pelletier formed a team in 1998. Two years later they came 4th at the Worlds and won the Canadian Championship with 5 perfect 6.0s. They returned to the Worlds in 2001, capturing the top title.

Salé and Pelletier skated a flawless long program in Salt Lake City and received an immediate standing ovation. Pelletier kissed the ice, the ecstatic crowd chanted "Six! Six! Six!" and CBC's Chris Cuthbert enthused, "One of the great skates in Olympic history!"

The scores came in placing the pair behind the flawed Russian performance. The shock was immediate, and Salé and Pelletier became front-page news and instant celebrities. After an investigation that led to a French judge being suspended for vote-swapping, Pelletier and Salé were awarded a shared gold medal with the Russians. The heroic pair turned professional following the Canada-wide, post-Olympic celebrations.

HONOURS

· *Soccer America* magazine's Freshman of the Year–2002

· WCC Player of the Year–2002, 2004, 2005

· M.A.C. Hermann Trophy–2004, 2005

· Canadian Player of the Year–2005, 2006, 2007, 2008, 2009

· Honda-Broderick Cup–2005

· WCC Female Scholar-Athlete of the Year–2006

· COSIDA Academic All-American of the Year–2006

· NSCAA/Adidas Female Scholar Athlete of the Year–2006

76 Christine Sinclair

1983 (Burnaby, British Columbia)–
STRIKER CHRISTINE SINCLAIR has done more than any other player to raise the profile of women's soccer in Canada. This skilled yet humble national team captain has a phenomenal 100-plus goals in a record 135-plus international games.

Sinclair was picked for B.C.'s under-14 team at only 11, and in 2000, at age 16, she joined the national senior team, where she has become a dominating force and team leader. Scoring 8 goals in 6 matches, Sinclair led Canada to a bronze medal at the 2007 Pan American Games, and at Beijing in 2008 she took Canada to the quarter-finals in their first-ever Olympic match.

Sinclair was also an outstanding U.S. collegiate player. In her first year at the University of Portland, she was league leader in goals, selected All-American, and named Freshman of the Year by *Soccer America* magazine. She was WCC Player of the Year an astonishing 3 times, 2-time winner of the prestigious M.A.C. Hermann Trophy, and an all-time record scorer with 39 goals. She also led her team to national championship victory twice, and was outstanding Collegiate Woman Athlete of the Year.

Currently playing for FC Gold Pride in the Women's Professional Soccer League, Sinclair likely has a long and storied soccer career ahead of her.

75 Gilles Villeneuve

1950 (Richelieu, Quebec)–1982
GILLES VILLENEUVE LAUNCHED his competitive career on the snow as a world champion snowmobile racer. His interest turned to auto racing, and he joined the Atlantic circuit in 1974, winning the series championship in 1976 and 1977.

Villeneuve's aggressive driving attracted Formula One attention, and in 1977 he joined the McLaren team. He switched to Ferrari—they were more comfortable with his reckless style—and claimed his first F-1 victory in front of an ecstatic hometown crowd at the 1978 Canadian Grand Prix in Montreal.

He won 3 races and finished 2nd overall in 1979, and in 1981 won twice and claimed a heroic 3rd at home, racing the final lap with a damaged car and limited vision.

Villeneuve—a fan favourite for being an intense risk taker on the track and a fun-loving gentleman off—started the 1982 season with the weight of expectation on his shoulders. At the qualifying race for the Belgian Grand Prix, just after setting a track record at a blistering 272 kilometres per hour, a vicious accident claimed his life. More than 25,000 mourners attended Villeneuve's funeral.

His son Jacques, who was only 11 when his father died, is also one of Canada's greatest auto racers.

HONOURS

· Order of the British Empire–1946
· Hockey Hall of Fame–1947
· Canada's Sports Hall of Fame–1975
· The Cyclone Taylor Award is awarded
  to the Vancouver Canucks MVP

74 Fred "Cyclone" Taylor

1883 (Tara, Ontario)–1979

VANCOUVER HOCKEY FANS bemoan never having won a Stanley Cup—but they're wrong. Hockey's first national superstar, the superb skater and defenceman-turned-forward Cyclone Taylor, led Vancouver to its one and only Cup victory.

The speedy forward grew up in Listowel, Ontario, playing junior and intermediate hockey. In the days before the NHL, Taylor played for 18 years as a professional in teams on both sides of the border and in several different leagues including the International Professional League, the National Hockey Association, and finally with the Pacific Coast Hockey Association.

Nicknamed "Cyclone" by Governor General Earl Grey, Taylor was famous from coast to coast for his hurricane speed and agility. Taylor led the Ottawa Senators of the NHA to a Stanley Cup in 1909, and was then paid a princely sum to move back west to join the Vancouver Millionaires of the PCHA. In 1915, in the first Stanley Cup played west of Winnipeg, Taylor scored 7 goals in 3 games to lead Vancouver to victory over Ottawa. He played for Vancouver for 9 years and repeatedly held the league scoring title. He retired from hockey in 1921.

HONOURS

· Canadian Boxing Hall of Fame–1955
· Canada's Sports Hall of Fame–1955
· Ring Boxing Hall of Fame–1960
· International Boxing Hall of Fame–1996
· Australian Boxing Hall of Fame–2009

73 Tommy Burns

1881 (Hanover, Ontario)-1955

NOAH BRUSSO, "THE Little Giant of Hanover," a.k.a. boxer Tommy Burns, is the only Canadian-born World Heavyweight Champion, and the first champion to travel the world to defend his title, succeeding against some of the fiercest fighters of his day.

Brusso changed his name to the Scottish-sounding Burns to hide his boxing habit from his mother. He started as a welterweight in 1900 at age 19. Six years later, the short, barrel-chested fighter with powerful shoulders and a sharp right punch challenged Marvin Hart, the World Heavyweight Champion. Burns—the 10-to-1 underdog—won the fight and fought 11 matches over the next 2 years to hold on to his WHC title.

In 1908 in Sydney, Australia, Burns became the first boxer to agree to a Heavyweight Championship with a black fighter—American Jack Johnson. Luckily for Burns, he had secured a guarantee of a rich win-or-lose purse prior to the fight because he lost to Johnson in a bloody 14-round battle that had to be stopped by the police.

Burns retired with an impressive record of 482 rounds in 57 fights with 34 knockouts, 5 losses, and 8 draws.

HONOURS

· Canada's Sports Hall of Fame–2005
· Canadian Olympic Hall of Fame–2005
· Governor General Meritorious Service
  Decoration–1994

72 Steve Bauer

1959 (St. Catharines, Ontario)- **STEVE BAUER CHANGED** the face of cycling in Canada. Nicknamed the "Fenwick Flash" after his hometown village of Fenwick, Ontario, Bauer joined the national cycling team in 1976, and in 7 years on the team was national road race champ 3 times.

He joined the international circuit, winning silver at the 1982 Commonwealth Games. At the 1984 Los Angeles Olympics, Bauer thrilled Canadians and surprised the Europeans, who dominated cycling, by capturing silver in the cycling road race event. This was Canada's first Olympic cycling medal since 1908.

Bauer turned professional after the Olympics, and immediately won bronze at the world cycling championship in Barcelona. He triumphed at numerous international races—first place in the 1986 and 1987 Grand Prix of Cycling, the 1988 Grand Prix d'Ameriques, the 1988 Tour de L'Oise, the 1988 Trofeo Pantalica, and the 1989 Zurich Championship. He also launched his Tour de France challenge and, in 1985, rode in his first of 11 Tour races. Bauer made his best appearance in 1988, when he won the first stage, wore the yellow jersey for 5 days, and finished 4th overall, setting a Canadian record. In 1990 he wore the yellow jersey again, this time for 9 days. He retired in 1996.

HONOURS

· CP Team of the Year–1998
· Canadian Curling Hall of Fame–1999
· Canada's Sports Hall of Fame–2000
· Canadian Olympic Hall of Fame–2005
· World Curling Freytag Award–2009

71 Sandra Schmirler

1963 (Biggar, Saskatchewan)–2000
"SCHMIRLER THE CURLER" was a dominant force in woman's curling in the 1990s. Born in the heart of curling country, Sandra Schmirler joined the local curling club at age 12 and played with the winning rink in the 1981 Saskatchewan high school curling championship. In 1987 she was part of her first provincial championship team.

After competing as third in the 1990 Saskatchewan championships, Schmirler formed her own rink, recruiting Jan Betker as third, Joan McCusker as second, and Marcia Gudereit as lead. This amazing foursome became the top rink in women's curling.

In 1993 the Schmirler rink won the Scott Tournament of Hearts—the Canadian Women's Curling Championship—followed by a gold medal win at the World Championships in Geneva. They repeated their wins in 1994 and again in 1997—the first time in curling history that a rink had won 3 world championship titles.

In 1998 the Schmirler rink made curling history. The sport became an official Olympic medal event in Nagano, and Canadians cheered as Schmirler's final phenomenal shot in the 10th end captured the world's first women's Olympic curling gold medal.

Schmirler died of breast cancer in 2000 at only 36.

70 Karen Magnussen

1952 (Vancouver, British Columbia)–
FIVE-TIME CANADIAN CHAMPION, Olympic silver medalist, and the last Canadian woman to win a World Figure Skating Championship, Karen Magnussen's achievements have gone unmatched for almost 4 decades.

Magnussen was a skating prodigy, winning the Canadian Juniors at 11 and Canadian Seniors at 14. At Grenoble in 1968, 15-year-old Magnussen was the youngest Canadian skater to attend an Olympics.

In 1969 Magnussen's skating future was in question. She developed painful stress fractures and required 3 months in leg casts, but made a remarkable comeback to win her second Canadian title. In 1971 she won the North American title and bronze at the Worlds, followed by silver at the 1972 Worlds.

Magnussen was instrumental in ushering in a new figure-skating era, with emphasis on free skating rather than compulsory figures. At the 1972 Olympics, figures counted for 50 percent of the overall score. Magnussen, in a stunning performance, won the free-skating event yet finished second overall. The Austrian skater, Beatrix Schuba was first in figures but finished 7th in the free skate yet she still captured gold. The following year figures were reduced to 30 percent and phased out entirely by the '90s.

At the 1973 World Championships, Magnussen clinched gold—something only 2 other Canadian women had done before and none has done since.

69 Kathy Kreiner

1957 (Timmins, Ontario)-
KATHY KREINER'S FATHER was team doctor at the 1968 Winter Olympics, and his exciting stories of Nancy Greene's heroic medal runs inspired the young skier. Following in the tracks of her new idol, Kreiner was winning important downhill races by age 7. She was asked to join the Canadian team at 14, and 2 years later, in 1974, she won her first World Cup gold medal in giant slalom.

Kreiner excelled over the next 2 years, preparing for the 1976 Olympics at Innsbruck where she would compete against her main rival, the multiple gold-medal winner Rosi Mittermaier from West Germany. Mittermaier was expected to win, but Kreiner was confidently preparing for something else. In the days before sport psychology and mental preparation were popular concepts, Kreiner spent hours developing her concentration. The combination of total focus and excellent athletic ability triumphed, and Kreiner took home Canada's only gold medal from those Games. At 18, she was the then-youngest skier ever to win Olympic gold.

In the next 5 years, Kreiner would claim 5 gold medals and 6 silver in national competitions, with an impressive 22 top-10 finishes in 62 World Cup races. Kreiner retired in 1981.

68 Nancy Garapick

1961 (Halifax, Nova Scotia)– SPUNKINESS, SPEED, AND youth were the features that set champion swimmer Nancy Garapick apart.

In 1973 she was youngest participant in the Canada Summer Games, at age 11. At 12, she captured her first national championship medal while setting 12 national age-group records and an astonishing 79 provincial records. At 13, she broke the world record in 200-metre backstroke at the Eastern Canadian Swimming Championships; the same year she won the Canadian title in 100- and 200-metre backstroke, and 2 months later she claimed silver and bronze medals in the same events at the 1975 World Aquatic Championships, where her main competitors were two East German powerhouses. While Garapick swam a record-breaking time in the 200-metre backstroke, she finished a scant 0.63 seconds behind East Germany's Birgit Treiber to win the silver.

A year later, Garapick was representing Canada again, this time at the Montreal Olympics. She took home 2 bronze medals and set an Olympic record in the heat for the 100-metre backstroke. Garapick started racing the individual medley and was soon the world's fastest in the 100 and 200 IM. In 9 years on the national team Garapick won 38 Canadian Championship medals, 17 national titles, and 60 medals in international competition.

HONOURS

- Bobbie Rosenfeld Award–1975
- Velma Springstead Award–1975
- Canadian Olympic Hall of Fame–1993
- Canada's Sports Hall of Fame–2008

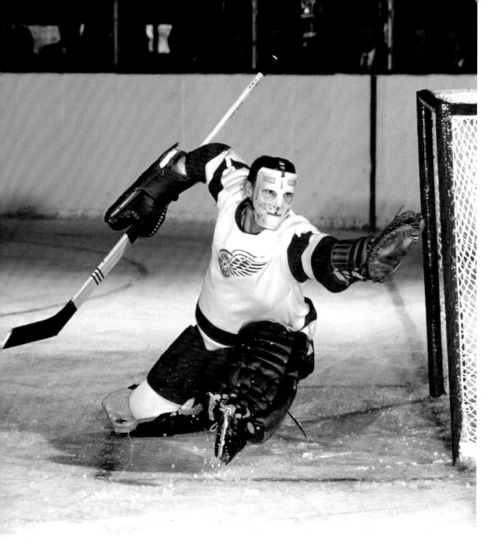

HONOURS

· Calder Trophy–1951

· Vezina Trophy–1952, 1953, 1955, 1965

· Lester Patrick Trophy–1971

· Hockey Hall of Fame–1971

· Canada's Sports Hall of Fame–1975

· Number 1 retired by Detroit Red Wings

67 Terry Sawchuk

1929 (Winnipeg, Manitoba)–1970

NHL GOALTENDER TERRY Sawchuk owned the crease for a remarkable 21 seasons and set the standard for professional goaltenders.

The 16-year-old goalie started playing for the junior Red Wings in 1946 and was called to the pros in 1950. In his first NHL season, Sawchuk dazzled Detroit fans by playing in every game (70) and recording the most wins in the league (44) while managing 11 shutouts and allowing a mere 1.99 goals per game. The next year the Calder trophy winner led his team to Stanley Cup victory, recording 4 shutouts in the playoffs alone and a remarkable 12 shutouts on the season.

Sawchuk backstopped 2 more Red Wing Cup victories in 3 years before being shipped to Boston in a surprising trade. He returned to Detroit in 1957, playing there for another 7 seasons before moving to Toronto, where he shared duties with the great Johnny Bower. He was in goal for the Leafs' Cup win in 1967, the same season he reached his 100th career shutout.

He retired in 1970 with a net-full of records, including most games (972), most minutes played (57,254), most wins (446), and most career shutouts (103)—one of the greatest goaltending careers of all time.

66 Phil Esposito

1942 (Sault Ste. Marie, Ontario)-
PHIL ESPOSITO DEVELOPED his scoring touch while taking shots on his brother Tony, a future NHL goaltender. He launched his NHL career in Chicago, but it wasn't until Esposito joined Bobby Orr and the Boston Bruins that his superstar career took off. In 1969, he became the first NHLer to reach 100 points in a season, and in 1971 he scored a remarkable 76 goals and 76 assists—a league record until Wayne Gretzky broke it in 1982. Esposito was the first to hit 5 straight 50-plus goal seasons (1970–75).

Esposito's emotional speech to Canadian fans during the historic 1972 Summit Series between Canada and Russia is legendary. Spectators had booed the failing Canadian team, and Esposito used a live TV interview to demand support from their country. The fans responded and filled the stands; the team responded with a heart-stopping, heroic victory. Esposito was the tournament's leading scorer with 7 goals and 6 assists.

In 1975, Esposito was traded to the New York Rangers. He continued to dominate, averaging a point a game.

Esposito's total goals (717) and points (1,590) were second on the books for many years. Over 18 seasons, the big forward represented Canada 3 times in international play. He also took home the Art Ross Trophy a remarkable 5 times.

HONOURS

· Hart Trophy–1928, 1931, 1932

· Hockey Hall of Fame–1945

· CP Outstanding Hockey Player of the Half-Century–1950

· Canada's Sports Hall of Fame–1955

· Number 7 retired by Montreal Canadiens

65 Howie Morenz

1902 (Mitchell, Ontario)–1937

WITH BLAZING SPEED and intense passion, Howie Morenz was the first NHL superstar.

In 1923 Morenz joined the Montreal Canadiens for their first-ever Stanley Cup–winning season, leading the team in playoff goals and finishing impressively high in league scoring.

Over the next 11 years, Morenz dominated the ice with his aggressive play and dazzling stickhandling, leading the Canadiens in scoring for 7 seasons, hoisting 2 more Stanley Cups, scoring 270 goals, and earning league MVP honours 3 times. In the 1929–30 season, he scored an astonishing 40 goals in 44 games.

In 1934 the Canadiens traded Morenz to Chicago, but in 1936 the "Canadiens Comet" returned to the *bleu, blanc, et rouge*. Canadiens fans were thrilled but soon devastated when, during a horrific on-ice accident, Morenz's leg was broken in 4 places. Two months later, while still recovering in hospital, Morenz died of a heart attack. He was only 34 years old.

Fifty thousand fans lined up at the Montreal Forum to pay respect to their hero, whose casket rested at centre ice. Thousands more across the country listened to the funeral service on their radios.

Morenz was the first player to have his sweater retired by the Canadiens.

64 Paul Coffey

1961 (Weston, Ontario)-
PAUL COFFEY WAS one of the most respected blueliners in NHL hockey, known for his lightning speed and bullet shot.

The Edmonton Oilers drafted Coffey in 1980 and launched his stellar career with an extraordinary collection of young teammates including Wayne Gretzky, Mark Messier, and Grant Fuhr.

In his rookie year, 19-year-old Coffey reached 32 points. The next season, with a spectacular 89 points, he was second in the NHL only to Gretzky. In 1984, when the high-flying Oilers took home their first Stanley Cup, he hit 126 points and won the Norris Trophy. This began Coffey's record-book domination with most goals, assists, and overall points by a defenceman in the playoffs, and most points by a defenceman in a single game. Coffey played a key role in the Oilers dynasty and 3 Cup-winning seasons.

In 1987, Coffey was traded to Pittsburgh where he played alongside newcomer Mario Lemieux. They led the team to its first Cup in 1991. He was traded to Los Angeles and then Detroit, where he earned his 3rd Norris Trophy. Bounced to 4 more teams, Coffey finished his 21-year career in Boston in 2001. His 1,531 career points was a league record for defencemen.

63 Daniel Nestor

1972 (Belgrade, Yugoslavia)–
DANIEL NESTOR, CANADA'S number-one tennis ace, is 1 of only 4 players in the world to win the Golden Grand Slam: Olympic gold plus all four tennis majors—the Australian, French, and U.S. Opens, and Wimbledon. Nestor, who played soccer and basketball as a boy, was hooked when he won his first tennis match at age 10, driven by visions of becoming the next Jimmy Connor.

With lightning-fast front-court exchanges, Nestor first sparked interest at the 1992 Davis Cup in Vancouver, where he beat number-one ranked Stefan Edberg. But doubles was Nestor's game. With partner Mark Knowles, he won his first title in 1994 against the reigning French Open champions. Nestor and Knowles, one of the most successful teams in tennis history, reached the Grand Slam finals 9 times and

won 3 majors—the 2002 Australian Open, 2004 U.S. Open, and 2007 French Open.

Nestor parted with Knowles in 2007 and joined Nenad Zimonjic, becoming the number-1 team on the 2008 tour and capturing Wimbledon in 2008 and 2009. He also clinched gold at the Sydney Olympics with partner Sébastien Lareau. Nestor has more than 60 doubles crowns; he is one of the world's top-ranked doubles player, 7-time Canadian Tennis Player of the Year, and 8-time Canadian Doubles Player of the Year.

HONOURS

· Wilson and McCall Trophy (with Sébastien Lareau)–2000
· ATP Doubles Team of the Year (with Mark Knowles) –2002, 2004, 2008
· Canadian Doubles Player of the Year–2002, 2003, 2004, 2005, 2006, 2007, 2008, 2009
· Canadian Tennis Player of the Year–2003, 2004, 2005, 2006, 2007, 2008, 2009

62 Ron Turcotte

1941 (Drummond, New Brunswick)-RON TURCOTTE—ONE OF the world's greatest jockeys—developed his special horse-rapport while guiding the family workhorse as she dragged logs through the New Brunswick bush.

Canada's winningest jockey in 1962 with 180 victories, Turcotte began racing in the U.S. on some of the greatest thoroughbreds in history. After his 1965 Preakness win riding Tom Rolfe, Turcotte became a regular in the American winner's circle. In 1972 he captured the Wood Memorial Stakes on Upper Case and both the Kentucky Derby and the Preakness Stakes on the colt Riva Ridge. But his record year was yet to come.

In 1973 Turcotte rode Secretariat—the greatest racehorse of all time—to a Triple Crown sweep—the first time in 25 years. His Kentucky Derby time and the 31-length win in the Belmont are standing records, and he was the first jockey in 64 years to win 2 Kentucky Derbies in a row and the only to have won 5 of 6 consecutive Triple Crown races.

Turcotte's riding career came to a tragic and abrupt end in 1978, when he was injured in a fall at Belmont Park that left him paralyzed from the waist down.

Over his 18-year career, Turcotte raced more than 20,000 mounts, won 3,032 times, and amassed over $28 million in earnings.

HONOURS

· Member of the Order of Canada–1974
· Sovereign Award, Man of the Year–1978
· George Woolf Jockey Award–1979
· National Horse Racing Hall of Fame–1979
· Canadian Horse Racing Hall of Fame–1980
· Canada's Sports Hall of Fame–1980
· Avelino Gomez Award–1984

HONOURS

· Lou Marsh Trophy–1978
· Norton H. Crow Award–1979
· John Semmelink Award–1980
· Canadian Olympic Hall of Fame–1984
· Canada's Sports Hall of Fame–1986
· Canadian Ski Hall of Fame–1987
· Member of the Order of Canada–1991
· Bruce Kidd Leadership Award–2001

61 Ken Read

1955 (Ann Arbor, Michigan)–
KEN READ, THE stalwart leader of the irrepressible "Crazy Canucks," dominated the ski slopes in the 1970s and '80s.

Read launched his bold career at Val d'Isère, France, in 1975 as the first non-European to win the men's World Cup downhill. He finished 5th at the 1976 Olympics in Innsbruck, and in 1978 captured the national Combined Event—downhill, slalom, and giant slalom. He landed 2 more World Cup honours, finishing 4th in overall World Cup standings 2 years in a row.

Read carried the flag for Canada at the Lake Placid Games in 1980, but lost a ski early in his race and didn't bring home a medal. That year he finished second in overall World Cup standings and spectacularly won 2 more World Cup races on notoriously difficult courses.

In his 9-year career, Read won 5 World Cup races, finishing 14 times in the top 3 and earning 36 top-10 honours. He was Canadian champion an amazing 5 times, a record made more outstanding by his formidable competitors, his Crazy Canucks teammates Steve Podborski, Dave Irwin, and Dave Murray.

60 Myriam Bédard

1969 (Neufchâtel, Quebec)–
MYRIAM BÉDARD'S EXCELLENCE in the winter biathlon earned her 3 Olympic medals and made this difficult sport, which combines cross-country skiing and target shooting, well-known across Canada.

Bédard learned to shoot and ski as a 15-year-old army cadet. She was Canadian Junior Champion from 1987 to 1989 and as a senior captured 3 gold, 2 silver, and 1 bronze medal at the 1991 World Cup. This left Bédard with a second-place ranking for the year, the highest ever by a North American in this European-dominated sport.

At the 1992 Games in Albertville, France—the first time women competed in the biathlon—Bédard won bronze in the 15-kilometre event becoming the first-ever Canadian Olympic biathlon medalist.

Four years later in Lillehammer, she thrilled spectators with an exhilarating gold-medal performance in the 15-kilometre. But Bédard's most memorable race was yet to come. Three days later in the 7.5-kilometre event, Bédard was a full 16 seconds behind the leader after 5 kilometres. She found the will to narrow the gap and with an extra push clinched the gold medal. This was the first double-gold performance by a Canadian woman in the Winter Olympics.

59 Johnny Longden

1907 (Wakefield, England)–2003
JOHNNY LONGDEN WAS born in Britain and died in the United States, but Canadian horse-racing fans proudly call him their own.

Longden developed his love for horses on the tracks near his adopted home of Calgary, and at 20 he left Canada with dreams of becoming a jockey. He spent most of his 40-year career in California, where he was 3-time leader in races won and twice leader in purse money.

Longden's greatest achievements came while riding Count Fleet. In 1943, they won the Triple Crown—the Kentucky Derby, the Preakness, and the Belmont Stakes; only 10 jockeys have reached this pinnacle. In 1956, Longden rode Arrogate to a record 4,871st win.

Longden's 6,000th career win was recorded in 1965 at Vancouver's Exhibition Park, atop Prince Scorpion. But his final race was one of his greatest. In 1966 at the San Juan Capistrano Handicap, Longden rode Canadian-bred George Royal from behind to a spectacular nose-victory, recording his 6,032nd win. George Royal had carried Longden to the Canadian International Championship a year earlier.

After he retired as the world's winningest rider, Longden trained horses; his Majestic Prince won the Kentucky Derby and the Preakness, making Longden the only person to both ride and train a Derby winner.

HONOURS

· National Museum of Racing and Hall of Fame–1958
· Canada's Sports Hall of Fame–1958
· Canadian Horse Racing Hall of Fame–1976
· Avelino Gomez Award–1985
· George Woolf Jockey Award–1952

HONOURS

· Lou Marsh Trophy—1954

· Bobbie Rosenfeld Award—1954, 1955

58 Marilyn Bell

1937 (Toronto, Ontario)–
HEROIC SWIMMER MARILYN BELL was competing in marathons by age 14. In 1954, the Canadian National Exhibition offered an American swimmer the vast sum of $10,000 to be the first to swim across Lake Ontario. Bell, already a celebrated amateur swimmer—just weeks before she'd been the first woman to complete the 42-kilometre (26-mile) Atlantic City marathon—considered this a snub to Canadian athletes. She announced that she would take on Lake Ontario at the same time—without pay.

Sixteen-year-old Bell launched her 51-kilometre (32-mile) swim in Youngstown, New York, just before midnight. Six hours later her American opponent, suffering from stomach pains, was forced to quit. Bell battled on through the bitterly cold water against brutal winds, 5-metre (16.5-foot) waves, and eels chomping at her heels. Canadians followed Bell's progress hour by hour on the radio and more than 100,000 cheering spectators greeted her on the shores of Lake Ontario. Bell had swum for an astounding 20 hours and 59 minutes. The CNE awarded her the money, and thousands of dollars in gifts poured in from adoring fans.

The next year Bell became the youngest swimmer to successfully cross the English Channel, and the following year she conquered the Strait of Juan de Fuca.

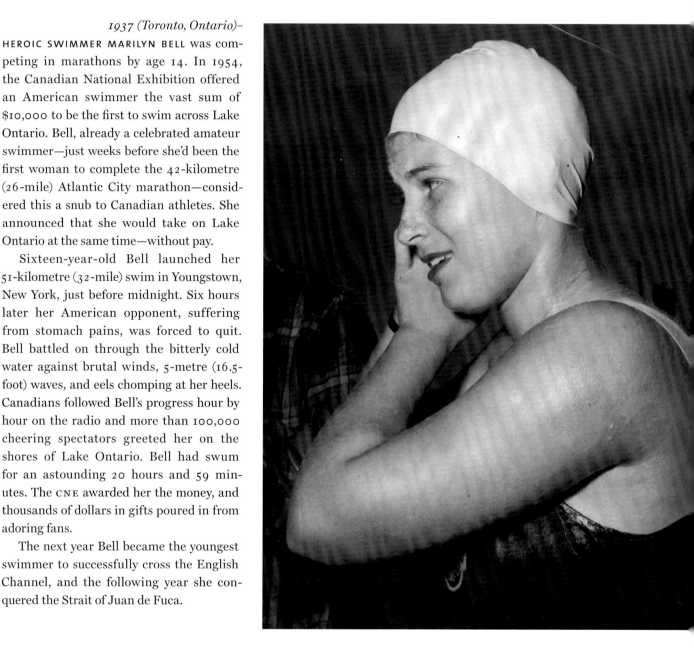

57 Eric Gagné

1976 (Montreal, Quebec)–
ERIC GAGNÉ'S NATURAL home was on the pitcher's mound. A Canadiens and Expos fan as a boy, and a star player with Canada's Junior World Championship team, Gagné became one of Major League Baseball's most outstanding relief pitchers.

Drafted by Chicago in 1994, a year later Gagné was the property of the Los Angeles Dodgers. He made his big-league debut in 1999 when the Dodgers recognized his true talent and switched him from starter to reliever. It wasn't until 2002, with 52 saves in 77 appearances, that his role as closer became solidified. With his scorching fastball and flummoxing change-up, Gagné topped the National League in 2003. With 55 saves and 137 strike-outs in 82 innings, Gagné claimed the Cy Young Award and became the first pitcher to record 50 saves in more than 1 season and the fastest pitcher to reach the 100-save plateau. His 55 saves equalled the National League record, and between August 2002 and July 2004, he converted 84 consecutive save chances—a Major League record.

In 2007 Gagne signed with the Texas Rangers, then was traded to the Boston Red Sox. The following season he signed with the Milwaukee Brewers, but because of a series of troubling injuries, one of the game's greatest closers has since been unable to earn a spot on an MLB roster.

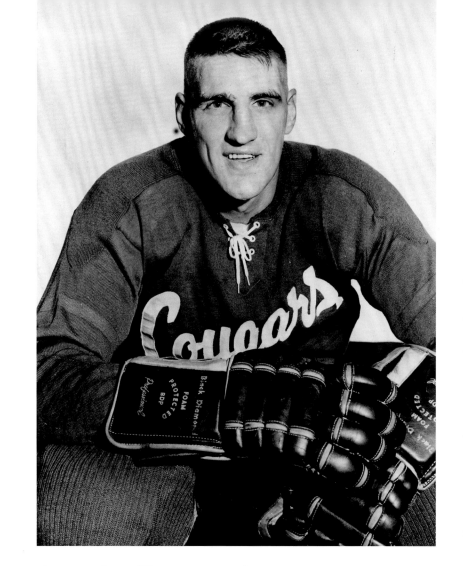

56 Jack Bionda

1933 (Huntsville, Ontario)–1999
JACK BIONDA EXCELLED in both of Canada's official sports, hockey and lacrosse, although his most spectacular achievements were with a lacrosse stick. With his deadly shot and lightning-fast reflexes, Bionda won the BC Senior A League scoring title 6 times in his 13-year career.

Bionda led Ontario's Brampton Excelsiors to the 1952 Minto Cup. Two years later he had moved to B.C., driving the Victoria Shamrocks to the 1954 Mann Cup and leading the league in scoring. He played for the New Westminster Salmonbellies and the Nanaimo Timbermen, reaching 7 Mann Cup finals and winning 5. In 1959

his points doubled those of his nearest competitor; he received the Commissioner's Trophy for MVP and the Mike Kelly Medal for Outstanding Player in the Mann Cup. He received the Kelly Medal again in 1962 when he had 16 points in 3 games while leading New Westminster to the Cup.

Bionda also spent time on the ice as a solid blueliner for the Toronto Maple Leafs (1955–1956) and the Boston Bruins (1956–59). He often missed important lacrosse games because of hockey commitments—lacrosse was his first love, but hockey paid his bills. He played 7 years for the Western Hockey League's Portland Buckaroos, taking the league championship twice.

55 Adam van Koeverden

1982 (Oakville, Ontario)–
SPRINT KAYAKER ADAM van Koeverden is a multiple Olympic-medal winner and a role model for kids who are not natural athletes. He admits, "I used to feel weird in gym class because I wasn't good at any sports." At 13 van Koeverden discovered kayaking and found his athletic groove.

By 17 he was competing internationally. He won bronze at the 1999 World Junior Championships, and in 2000 was world junior marathon champion. In 2001 he won World Cup silver in the 200-metre, and in 2003 he claimed his first World Championship silver in the 1000-metre.

Canadians remember van Koeverden's exciting performance at the 2004 Olympics in Athens. First he won bronze in the 1000-metre event. Three days later, in what van Koeverden called "the perfect race," he captured 500-metre gold to claim the first double-medal win for Canada in the Summer Olympics since 1996. He was proud flag bearer at the Closing Ceremonies, and returned to a hero's welcome.

Van Koeverden continued to win world championships over the next 3 years—he's got 16 on his résumé—and was a favourite—and flag bearer again—going into the 2008 Beijing Olympics. He seized the silver medal in the 500-metre event, breaking his own world-record time.

54 Steve Yzerman

1965 (Cranbrook, British Columbia)- STEVE YZERMAN WAS the Detroit Red Wings' first-round draft selection in 1983, and he scored more points and more assists than any other rookie while carrying his team into the playoffs for the first time in 6 years.

Yzerman was named captain in 1986 at only 21 years old—the youngest in franchise history. In 1988–89, he scored points in 70 of his 80 regular season games, posted a career-high 65 goals and 90 assists, and was 3rd in the league scoring race behind Gretzky and Lemieux. In 1993 he posted his 6th consecutive 100-plus points season.

Yzerman scored his 500th goal in 1996, and racked up 20 points in 18 playoff games. The next season he led the Red Wings in their triumphant run to the Stanley Cup— their first in 4 decades. He repeated the triumph the next season, and in 2002 he captained the Wings to their 3rd Cup in six years, becoming 1 of only 3 players to win the Stanley Cup and Olympic gold medal in the same year.

"The Captain" retired in 2006 leading the Wings in assists, ahead of Gordie Howe, and as the longest-serving captain in NHL history. Yzerman touched gold again in 2010, as Executive Director of Team Canada at the Vancouver Olympics.

HONOURS

· Lester B. Pearson Award–1989
· Conn Smythe Trophy–1998
· Frank J. Selke Trophy–2000
· Bill Masterton Trophy–2003
· Lester Patrick Trophy–2006
· Canada's Sports Hall of Fame–2008
· Hockey Hall of Fame–2009
· Number 19 retired by Detroit Red Wings

53 Ian Millar

1947 (Halifax, Nova Scotia)–
IN THE REFINED world of equestrian show jumping, Ian Millar soars. The most decorated equestrian in Canadian history, Millar has been at the forefront of Canadian show jumping for almost 4 decades.

Millar developed his passion for riding early, practising on the family piano bench before he rode his first horse. He made the Canadian Equestrian team in 1971 and has since won a record 10 Canadian Show Jumping Championships.

Millar's greatest victories came with one horse, the legendary Big Ben. Together they represented Canada on 7 winning Nations Cup teams and were the first horse-and-rider combination to win back-to-back World Cup finals in 1988 and 1989. Millar and Big Ben claimed more than 40 Grand Prix victories, including two at Spruce Meadows—the world's richest Grand Prix event. Together the successful duo won more than $1.5 million in prize money (Millar's career total to date is more than $2.2 million).

Millar has competed in 9 Olympics—a world record in any sport. At the 2008 Beijing Games, 61-year-old Millar, on his mount In Style, anchored the Canadian team to a silver medal. Millar intends to compete for Canada with his son and daughter in the 2012 London Olympics.

HONOURS

· Lester B. Pearson Award–1989
· Member of the Order of Canada–1986
· Canadian Olympic Hall of Fame–1990
· Canada's Sports Hall of Fame–1996

52 Sandra Post

1948 (Oakville, Ontario)-
SANDRA POST SWUNG her first golf club at age 5 and—even though her first love was figure skating—developed a life-long fascination for the green. The great tee-master became Ontario's Junior Champion at 15 and National Junior Champion at 16—she went on to win both titles 3 times. She turned professional at 19, and 6 months later shocked the golf world by beating the great Kathy Whitworth to become both the youngest and the first non-American LPGA Champion.

After her stellar start—Post was LPGA and *Golf Digest* Rookie of the Year for 1968—she battled for most of the 1970s to regain her exalted position. In 1978 and 1979 she made a spectacular comeback by winning the Dinah Shore Open 2 years in a row—the first to capture back-to-back victories in this prestigious event. Post was at the top of the game for the next few seasons with 7 wins from 1978 to 1982.

Post retired from professional competition in 1984. In her 16-year professional career, she won 8 LPGA tournaments—still the most by any Canadian—with 20 second-place finishes, including one at the challenging U.S. Women's Open.

51 George Knudson

1937 (Winnipeg, Manitoba)–1989
GEORGE KNUDSON, CANADA'S legendary "King of Swing," ruled the links for more than a decade. A remarkable technician, Knudson's consistently perfect swing drove him to multiple national and international titles and put Canada on the international golfing map.

At age 17 Knudson earned Manitoba's junior title in 1954. The next year he repeated the performance and won the Canadian junior title. Three years later he turned professional, and in 1961 joined the PGA tour, claiming a victory in his first year at the Coral Gables Open. He played the professional circuit for 11 years, capturing 8 tournament victories—the most ever by a Canadian golfer—with 1 World Cup win in 1968.

Knudson won 5 CPGA titles, was low Canadian professional in 5 Canadian Opens, and was 1 stroke away from the 1969 Masters.

Renowned for his machine-like stroke, Knudson shared his skills through a variety of teaching endeavours, including books, videos, and the CPGA teaching manual. He died of lung cancer in 1989 at only 52 years old. In 1999, he was named Golfer of the Twentieth Century by the Canadian Professional Golf Association.

50 Rick Hansen

1957 (Port Alberni, British Columbia)–
EVEN BEFORE HIS heroic "Man in Motion" tour, Rick Hansen was one of Canada's most outstanding athletes. With his world wheelchair marathon he became one of the most extraordinary.

Growing up in Williams Lake, B.C., Hansen was a natural sportsman. At 15, he was thrown from the back of a pick-up truck and paralyzed from the waist down. After months of rehabilitation, he trained intensively in wheelchair athletics and was soon winning national and international competitions in both team and individual sports.

Hansen was a gifted competitor, excelling at racquetball and tennis and playing on national champion wheelchair volleyball and basketball teams. An exceptional marathoner, he won an astounding 19 international wheelchair marathons. At the 1982 Pan American Wheelchair Games, Hansen raced to 9 gold medals and 9 records; that same year he placed first (unofficially) in the Boston Marathon. At the 1984 Paralympic Games, Hansen captured 2 gold medals (1,500-metre and marathon) and 1 silver (5,000-metre); he won gold and silver at the 1984 World Wheelchair Games.

Hansen's 40,000-kilometre, 2-year round-the-globe wheelchair marathon inspired the world. From March 1985 to May 1987, he covered the equivalent of 3 marathons each day, travelling through 34 countries to raise more than $26 million for spinal cord research.

HONOURS

· National Disabled Athlete of the Year–1979, 1980, 1982
· Lou Marsh Trophy–1983
· Companion of the Order of Canada–1988
· British Columbia Wheelchair Sports' Athlete of the Century–2000
· Canada's Sports Hall of Fame–2006

49 Jean Béliveau

1931 (Trois-Rivières, Quebec)– AT THE HEART of the Montreal Canadiens hockey dynasty of the 1950s and '60s skated the gentlemanly figure of Jean Béliveau. Young Béliveau's skills attracted early attention. At 15, the powerful skater signed with the Montreal Canadiens, agreeing to play for them when he turned professional. He wouldn't be rushed—as lead scorer in the Quebec Senior League he was content to remain amateur. Determined Canadiens management went to the extraordinary length of buying Béliveau's team and turning it professional. He reluctantly joined the Habs in 1953.

Béliveau used his size and strength to execute elegantly brilliant plays. In 1956, on the legendary line with Maurice Richard and Bert Olmstead, he led the Habs to the first of 5 consecutive Stanley Cups (he won 7 in all as a player). He won the Art Ross, Hart, and Lionel Conacher trophies that year.

Béliveau's name is on the Stanley Cup 17 times—more than any other—reflecting his years as a player and team executive. In 1965 he was the first player to win the Conn Smythe Award and he's second behind Guy Lafleur as the Canadiens' all-time scoring leader. Béliveau's 10-sesaon tenure as captain is the longest in Habs history.

48 Elaine Tanner

1951 (Vancouver, British Columbia)–
ELAINE TANNER HAD earned 17 Canadian
swimming championships by age 17. In
1966 she dominated the Commonwealth
Games in Jamaica, claiming 4 gold, 3 silver,
and 2 world records. That year she received
the Bobbie Rosenfeld Award and was the
youngest athlete ever to receive the Lou
Marsh Trophy.

At the 1967 Pan American Games in
Winnipeg, Tanner captured gold in the 100-
and 200-metre backstroke, setting world
records in both, and adding 3 silver for good
measure. That outstanding performance
earned the diminutive swimmer the adoration of Canadian fans and the nickname
"Mighty Mouse."

Canada had not won Olympic swimming
gold since 1928, and heavy expectations
weighed on the young athlete going into
the 1968 Games. Tanner broke the Olympic
record in the 100-metre backstroke, but
the American swimmer was faster—Tanner finished second. She left those Games
with 3 medals: 2 silver and a bronze—an
outstanding achievement at any Olympics
and particularly impressive when the entire
Canadian Olympic team won only 5 medals.
But Tanner was devastated at losing gold
and returned home to a disappointed and
critical public. She retired from swimming
the next year at only 18 years old and is still
one of the most successful female swimmers
in Canadian history.

47 Beckie Scott

1974 (Vegreville, Alberta)–
BECKIE SCOTT, NORTH America's most-decorated cross-country skier, has the rare distinction of claiming Olympic bronze, silver, and gold for a single race.

Scott started skiing for Canada in 1994 and raced at Nagano in 1998. At the Salt Lake City Olympics in 2002, a dramatic finish-line lunge earned Scott bronze—the first North American to win an Olympic cross-country medal. But in the months to follow, testing revealed that some of Scott's competitors—including the first- and second-place Russian skiers—were using banned substances. Scott was awarded silver. Two years after the initial podium ceremony her medal was officially upgraded to its true colour; she accepted her gold medal on the steps of the Vancouver Art Gallery.

Even before Salt Lake City, Scott had been disturbed by the prevalence of doping at the highest levels of cross-country skiing. Determined to clean up her sport, she started a campaign. Her complaints fell on deaf ears, until her bronze-medal finish led to the gold medal she clearly—and cleanly—earned.

In 2005 and 2006 Scott managed phenomenal seasons with a second-place overall standing and 10 World Cup podium finishes. At the Turin Olympics, Scott and partner Sara Renner won silver in the team sprint. In 2 decades of international competition, she won 17 World Cup medals.

46 George Chuvalo

1937 (Toronto, Ontario)- **GEORGE CHUVALO, CANADA'S** boxing champ for 18 years, ranked in the world heavyweight top-10 longer than any other fighter. This big-hearted and fiercely determined boxer stayed on his feet for every one of his 97 professional fights.

Chuvalo first entered the ring at age 10. At 18 he represented Canada at the 1956 Olympics, but a lack of funds forced him to turn pro. In 1958, he claimed his first Canadian heavyweight title and turned his eyes to the big prize—World Heavyweight Champion. An old-style fighter with a granite chin, he rose to number-2 fighter in the world by 1962. He lost 2 big fights (against Floyd Patterson and Ernie Tyrell) by close decisions and in 1966 shared the ring with the great Muhammad Ali. It was a bone-crushing battle—Ali said, "He was the toughest man I ever fought"—but after 15 rounds Chuvalo lost by decision. In a rematch in 1972 Chuvalo went the distance but again lost by decision.

Chuvalo retired in 1979 with an astonishing 73 wins (including 64 knockouts), 18 losses and 2 draws.

HONOURS
· Canada's Sports Hall of Fame–1990
· World Boxing Hall of Fame–1997
· Member of the Order of Canada–1998

45 Silken Laumann

1964 (Mississauga, Ontario)-
SILKEN LAUMANN'S BRONZE-MEDAL performance at the 1992 Olympics stands as one of the most triumphant moments in Canadian sports.

Laumann joined the National Team in 1983 and within 2 years was winning international competitions, including a gold at the U.S. Championships, gold at the Pan American Games, and her first Olympic medal—a bronze in double sculls, paired with her sister—at the 1984 Games.

Laumann's success continued—Pan American gold in 1987; silver at the 1990 Worlds; gold at the 1991 Worlds. Olympic gold seemed secure at the upcoming Barcelona Games. But just weeks before Barcelona, at a warm-up race in Germany,

Laumann's shell was broadsided by a German boat. Her injuries were devastating and, according to her doctors, would end her rowing career. Five operations and 3 weeks later, a tenacious Laumann stepped from a wheelchair into her racing shell and— even though she couldn't walk—started rowing. With 5 weeks until the Olympics, Laumann launched into a vigorous training regimen. In a dramatic finish, the would-be world champion raced from career-ending injury to Olympic glory, her bronze medal an unmatchable achievement.

Laumann continued to compete internationally, winning silver at the 1995 Worlds and silver again at the Olympics in 1996. She retired in 1999.

HONOURS

· Canadian Olympic Hall of Fame–1963
· Officer of the Order of Canada–1971
· Canada's Sports Hall of Fame–1971
· British Columbia's Athlete of the Century–1999

44 Harry Jerome

1940 (Prince Albert, Saskatchewan)–1982
DESPITE A SPATE of severe injuries, Harry Jerome was at the top of the track world for almost a decade. A talented athlete on the baseball and football fields, Jerome became known for his unmatched speed on the track. At 18, he smashed Percy William's 220-yard (200-metre) national record and the next year tied the 100-metre world record, but his hopes for the 1960 Rome Olympics were dashed by injury.

Jerome attended the University of Oregon on a track scholarship, anchoring the school's relay team to a world record. But at the 1962 Commonwealth Games he finished last in the 100-metre after suffering a severed quadriceps mid-race. Despite the severity of the damage—his surgeon declared Jerome would never run again—the media dubbed Jerome a quitter. He returned after 1 year and—bearing a 30-centimetre (almost 1-foot) scar on his thigh—ran brilliantly to 100-metre bronze at the 1964 Olympics in Tokyo. He finished a respectable 4th in the 200-metre race, laying to rest the media's judgments.

Jerome, who set 7 world records, retired in 1968 after competing in his 3rd Olympics. The prestigious Harry Jerome International Track Classic is held each year in Burnaby, B.C.

43 Brian Orser

1961 (Belleville, Ontario)-
TWO-TIME OLYMPIC SILVER medalist Brian Orser is one of Canada's most decorated figure skaters.

In 1979 Orser nabbed the national Junior Men's Championship in a spectacular performance, becoming the first junior to land a triple axel in competition. Two years later he launched a succession of national titles—he won 7 in total—earning the title "Mr. Triple Axel" for his consistent success with this difficult and crowd-pleasing jump. A natural showman, Orser dazzled judges with his powerful and dynamic performances.

At the 1984 Sarajevo Olympics, Orser scored silver—at that time, the best-ever Olympic performance by a Canadian male skater. In 1985 he won his 5th straight national title with the highest marks ever awarded in that competition.

In 1987 Orser triumphed with an outstanding performance at the Worlds—7 triple jumps including 2 triple axels. This remarkable gold-medal performance was another Canadian first.

Orser carried the Canadian flag into the Calgary Olympics in 1988. On the ice, he missed gold by a fraction of a point to American rival Brian Boitano. The 1988 Worlds—another "Battle of the Brians"—ended with similar results.

At the 2010 Games in Vancouver, Orser finally enjoyed Olympic gold victory as coach of the phenomenal Yu-Na Kim of Korea.

42 Kathleen Heddle

1965 (Trail, British Columbia)–
WORLD CHAMPION ROWER Kathleen Heddle's private nature has meant she is not as well known as her gregarious crewmate Marnie McBean, although she was the calm strength behind the most decorated Olympic pair in Canadian history.

Heddle started rowing for the University of British Columbia at age 19 and rapidly rose to national-team level and a gold medal at the 1987 Pan Am Games in straight pairs.

Reserved Heddle was matched with extroverted McBean, who quickly came to appreciate Heddle's exceptional talent. In 1991 the duo won gold in pairs and eights and set a world record at the World Championships. The extraordinary pair went on to Olympic gold in Barcelona in 1992, and a second gold medal with the women's eight.

Heddle left rowing after 1992, but McBean persuaded her to return for the 1996 Atlanta Games. The reigning Olympic champions faced constant media scrutiny. Heddle relied on McBean to be spokeswoman, while McBean looked to Heddle to keep them focused on racing. The rowing "odd couple" captured gold in the doubles skull becoming the first Canadian Summer Olympians to win 3 gold medals, then added bronze in quad sculls to make them Canada's most successful Olympic pairs team.

HONOURS
· Canadian Olympic Hall of Fame–1994
· Wilson and McCall Trophy (with Marnie McBean) –1995, 1996
· Canada's Sports Hall of Fame–1997
· Thomas Keller Medal–1999

HONOURS

· Lou Marsh Trophy–1973, 1976
· Member of the Order of Canada–1976
· George Woolf Jockey Award–1976
· Canada's Horse Racing Hall of Fame–1986
· Avelino Gomez Award–1986
· Sovereign Award, Outstanding Jockey–1978, 1988
· Sovereign Award, Man of the Year–1988
· National Thoroughbred Racing Hall of Fame–1992
· Canada's Sports Hall of Fame–1998

41 Sandy Hawley

1949 (Oshawa, Ontario)–
SANDY HAWLEY—CANADA'S greatest jockey—spent his late teens hot-walking horses at Toronto's tracks. In 1968 he became a regular rider, winning his first race at Woodbine. Within a year, Hawley was North America's number 1 apprentice jockey, leading in wins for 4 of the next 6 years. In 1973 he won 515 races, becoming the first jockey to win 500 races in 1 year.

In 1972 Hawley moved to California where he thrived in the rich riding culture. In 1976 he received the prestigious George Woolf Memorial Jockey Award for his high standard of personal and professional conduct both on and off the racetrack—Hawley was considered to be one of the greatest gentlemen in the sport. That same year he broke thoroughbred racing's all-time money-winning record for a single year and won North America's most outstanding jockey award.

Hawley reached his 5,000th career win in 1986—the youngest jockey to reach that plateau. He returned to Ontario in 1988, and won his 6,000th race in 1992.

By the end of his 31-year career, Hawley had recorded 6,449 wins on 31,455 mounts and claimed the Queen's Plate—Canada's most prestigious thoroughbred horse race—4 times.

40 Caroline Brunet

1969 (Quebec City, Quebec)-
KAYAKING LEGEND CAROLINE Brunet started racing at 11, and was only 18 when she entered her first Olympics at Seoul in 1988. She reached 7th at the 1992 Games in Barcelona and, after a tough training regimen with a new coach, grabbed silver at Atlanta in 1996.

Brunet's next few years of international competition were exemplary. Triple world champion in 1997 and 1999 (winning gold in K-1 200, 500 and 1,000 metres), and double world champ in 1998. She was awarded Canadian Athlete of the Year in 1999.

Brunet proudly carried the flag into the 2000 Games at Sydney. Expectations were high for kayaking gold, but gusting winds and rough water led to a 5-hour delay in the

K-1 500 final. Despite the distractions Brunet raced to a silver-medal finish.

At Athens in 2004, 35-year-old Brunet won a bronze medal, making her one of the few elite Canadian athletes to bring home individual medals from 3 consecutive Olympics.

Brunet retired with 21 ICF Canoe Sprint World Championship medals (10 gold, 7 silver, and 4 bronze).

HONOURS

· Velma Springstead Award–1997, 1999, 2000
· Lou Marsh Trophy–1999
· Canada's Sports Hall of Fame–2009

39 Marc Gagnon

1975 (Chicoutimi, Quebec)–
RETIREMENT IS ONE of the hardest decisions
world-class athletes face. Short-track speed
skating superstar Marc Gagnon almost
made his decision too early.

Gagnon was born into speed skating—as
a toddler he played at the ice rink where his
parents taught skating. By age 14 Gagnon's
talent was evident and at 17 he won his first
world title. For the next decade Gagnon was
top in the sport—4-time World Champion
and winner of 2 Olympic medals, a bronze
in Lillehammer, and relay gold in Nagano.

At Nagano Gagnon had been disqualified
from the 1,000-metre event and fallen during the 500. He left those Games unhappy,
lamenting, "I was disappointed enough to
believe that I was done with speed skating."

But Gagnon wasn't finished after all. A
year later he announced his comeback and
turned his sights to the 2002 Olympics
in Salt Lake City. A bronze-medal performance in the 1,500-metre boosted Gagnon's
confidence. He prepared for the 500 and, in
a dramatic come-from-behind performance,
reached gold. A second gold came only 90
minutes later as he anchored the 5,000-
metre relay team to his 5th Olympic medal,
becoming the most-decorated Canadian
athlete in Winter Olympic history (surpassed in 2006 by fellow speed skater Cindy
Klassen)—an enormous achievement that
almost wasn't.

HONOURS

· Canadian Olympic Hall of Fame–2007
· Canada's Sports Hall of Fame–2008

38 Mark Messier

1961 (Edmonton, Alberta)– ASIDE FROM HAVING more career points than any player in NHL history—except Gretzky—Mark Messier is renowned for his strength, passion, and invaluable leadership abilities.

With a hockey-playing father, Messier grew up on the rink. At 16 and already 200 pounds, the strong, talented skater—nicknamed "the Moose"—tried out with the WHA. After a season with the Indianapolis Racers and the Cincinnati Stingers, Messier was drafted in 1979 to the NHL by his hometown Edmonton Oilers.

Messier was a star presence with the Oilers during their glory years of the late '80s and a driving force behind the dynasty's 4 Stanley Cups in 5 years (1984–88). He won the Conn Smythe Trophy in 1984 and in 1990 captained the Oilers to their 5th Cup. He was traded to the New York Rangers in 1991 and led that franchise to its first Stanley Cup in 54 years.

Messier represented Canada at 3 Canada Cup Tournaments, 1 World Championship, and 1 World Cup. In 1998 he scored his 600th career goal and in 2004 he surpassed Gordie Howe's career points. Messier—one of the greatest players and leaders in the game—retired with 1,887 career points (694 goals, 1,193 assists).

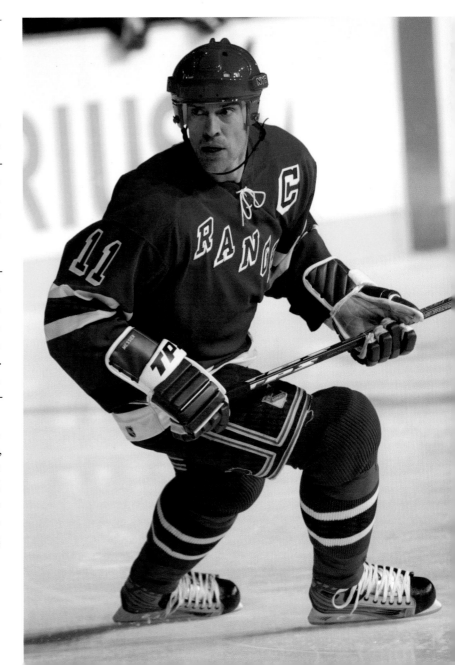

HONOURS

· Conn Smythe Trophy–1986, 1993, 2001
· William M. Jennings Trophy–1987, 1988, 1989,
  1992, 2002
· Vezina Trophy–1989, 1990, 1992
· Trico Goaltending Award–1989, 1990
· Hockey Hall of Fame–2006
· Number 33 retired by Colorado Avalanche
  and Montreal Canadiens

37 Patrick Roy

1965 (Sainte-Foy, Quebec)-
FOR **19 SEASONS**, the legendary Patrick Roy dominated the NHL with his amazing reflexes, fiery personality, and uncanny ability to play under pressure. Roy popularized Glenn Hall's butterfly style of goaltending while breaking records and leading his teams to 4 Stanley Cups.

Roy led the Sherbrooke Canadiens to their only Calder Cup Championship in 1985. In 1986, the 20-year-old Montreal Canadiens rookie posted an exceptional 1.92 goals-against average in 20 playoff games to become the youngest Conn Smythe winner in NHL history. Roy—dubbed "Saint Patrick"—received a hero's welcome in Montreal.

Roy won his second Conn Smythe in the 1993 Stanley Cup series against the Gretzky-led Los Angeles Kings. Two years later and after 11 seasons with the Canadiens, Roy joined the Colorado Avalanche and helped lead that team to their first Stanley Cup. In the 2000–01 playoffs, Roy performed brilliantly for the Avalanche to finish with a goals-against average of 1.70 and a .934 save percentage to earn his 3rd Conn Smythe and his 4th Stanley Cup.

When he retired in 2003, Roy was the NHL's all-time leading goalie in career wins (551) and games played (1,029), and holder of several playoff records.

HONOURS

· Canada's Sports Hall of Fame–1955
· Canadian Olympic Hall of Fame–1960
· The Tom Longboat Award is awarded to Canada's
  top male and female Aboriginal athlete
· *Maclean's Magazine*'s Canadian sports figure of the
  20th century–1999

36 Tom Longboat

1887 (Six Nations Reserve, Ontario)–1949
AT THE TURN of the 20th century, the most famous Canadian athletes weren't hockey players but runners. Marathoner and world champion Tom Longboat was Canada's greatest.

Longboat entered his first 5-mile (8-kilometre) race at 18. Two years later he won the 1907 Boston Marathon, smashing the previous record by an astounding 5 minutes. He enjoyed a hero's welcome on his return to Toronto—he was given the keys to the city and promised $500 for his education (which he never received, although the money plus interest was eventually given to his children in 1980).

Longboat's training schedule of alternating strenuous and light workouts is considered progressive today but was unusual at the turn of the last century, and some trainers and journalists called him lazy. But spectators loved to watch Longboat's long stride and explosive finishes, and after Boston and a season of record-breaking races, he was favoured to win at the 1908 Olympics. Longboat collapsed in the sweltering heat and was carried off at mile 20.

Longboat turned professional and competed in a series of one-on-one races at Madison Square Garden against the leaders from the 1908 Olympics. In the final match, in front of a standing-room-only crowd, he pulled ahead of Englishman Alfie Shrubb, in the last mile, to become Marathon Champion of the World.

35 Justin Morneau

1981 (New Westminster, British Columbia)– MAJOR LEAGUE BASEBALL star Justin Morneau came close to choosing hockey as his preferred profession. At 17, the young athlete was 3rd goalie for the Portland Winter Hawks of the WHL. Rather than wait for more ice time, Morneau turned his focus to his other passion: baseball.

Moreau had played on the national team in 1997 and 1998, winning Best Hitter and Best Catcher honours in the National Championships. In 1999 the Minnesota Twins took notice, and he made his major league debut in June 2003 at age 22.

Morneau claimed his spot as the Twins' starting first baseman in 2004. In 2006 his team-leading 34 homeruns and league-second 130 RBIS led to the American League MVP Award—making him the first Canadian player to win this honour.

Morneau signed a 6-year, $80-million contract in 2008, the longest and richest contract in Twins history. He had a stellar season with a career-high 5-hit game and a respectable 23 homeruns and 129 RBIS. In September 2009, a stress fracture in his back forced Morneau to hang up his glove for the remainder of the season. This 3-time All-Star may just be reaching his peak as he continues his impressive MLB run.

34 Bobby Hull

1939 (Pointe Anne, Ontario)-
FLAMBOYANT AND FAST, the Golden Jet changed the face of the NHL with his powerful slapshot and muscular play.

Bobby Hull joined the Chicago Black Hawks in 1957. The rookie left-winger started slow—13 goals in his first season, 18 the second. The next season, Hull captured the league scoring title with 81 points and 39 goals, and Chicago took home the Stanley Cup for the first time in 23 years.

In 1961-62 Hull tallied 50 goals and 84 points, winning the scoring title a second time. In 1966 he became the first player to score more than 50 goals in a season, finishing with a record 54 goals and 97 points for his 3rd Art Ross Trophy.

In 1972 Hull reached the 50-goal plateau for an astonishing 5th time, and the Winnipeg Jets of the WHA came calling. Hull couldn't refuse their million-dollar offer, and by fall he was scoring in the new league. His extravagant contract changed the way hockey players were paid.

Hull shone in the WHA—he was league MVP in 1973 and 1975. Hull retired with 610 goals in 1,063 regular-season games. Bobby and his son Brett are the only father-son duo with their names on the Hart and Lady Byng trophies.

HONOURS

· Art Ross Trophy—1960, 1962, 1966
· Lady Byng Trophy—1965
· Hart Trophy—1965, 1966
· Lionel Conacher Award—1965, 1966
· Lester Patrick Trophy—1969
· Officer of the Order of Canada—1978
· Hockey Hall of Fame—1983
· Canada's Sports Hall of Fame—1988
· Number 9 retired by Chicago Black Hawks and Winnipeg Jets

33 Victor Davis

1964 (Guelph, Ontario)–1989

INTENSE AND PASSIONATE, swimming champion Victor Davis was driven to win.

Davis learned to swim in Ontario's lakes and started swimming competitively at 12. In 1981, at 17, he won gold in the 100-metre breaststroke at the Canadian Nationals—the first of a phenomenal 31 national titles.

At his first international competition—the World Championships in Guayaquil, Ecuador, in 1982—Davis set a world record on his way to the gold medal. Shortly after, at the Commonwealth Games in Australia, Davis hit gold and silver in the 200-metre and 100-metre breaststroke.

At the Los Angeles Olympics in 1984, Davis won gold in the 200-metre breaststroke in world-record time, grabbed silver in the 100-metre breaststroke, and was key to the 4×100-metre relay team's silver—a remarkable achievement given that his training regime had been significantly compromised due to mononucleosis the year before.

Davis' domination continued with 2 more golds and 1 silver at the 1986 Commonwealth Games and a gold and silver at the Worlds. With a silver medal from Seoul in 1988 (in the 4×100-metre medley relay), Davis had more Olympic medals than any other Canadian swimmer. He retired the following year at age 25. Only months later, Victor Davis was killed in a car accident.

HONOURS

· Swimming Canada's Athlete of the Year–1982, 1984, 1986
· Member of the Order of Canada–1984
· Canadian Olympic Hall of Fame–1985
· Canada's Sports Hall of Fame–1990
· International Swimming Hall of Fame–1994

32 Elvis Stojko

1972 (Newmarket, Ontario)-
WHEN ELVIS STOJKO burst onto the figure skating scene at age 17, the world took notice. His strength, explosive power, and unmatched jumping ability combined for a groundbreaking, tremendously exciting, yet controversial performance.

Stojko trained in both figure skating and karate, earning his black belt by 16. On ice, in contrast to traditional fashion, Stojko performed to energetic beats with robust martial arts–inspired moves in black outfits emphasizing his muscular physique. His unorthodox style was celebrated by fans but challenged judges.

Stojko's technical achievements were unmatched—the first to land a quadruple-double jump combination and a quadruple-triple combination—yet he consistently received low scores for artistic presentation. Many believe the judges robbed Stojko of a gold medal at the 1994 Olympics. He took home silver, but had won gold earlier that year for the identical routine at the World Championships in Japan.

Stojko became a national hero after his silver win at Nagano in 1998. He suffered a severe groin injury before the final program. Doubled over in pain after his long program, Stojko limped onto the podium to accept his heroically earned medal.

With 3 World and 7 Canadian titles, as well as 2 Olympic silver medals, Stojko changed the aesthetic of the sport forever.

HONOURS

· Lionel Conacher Award–1994
· Norton H. Crow Award–1994, 1997
· Canada's Sports Hall of Fame–2006

31 Martin Brodeur

1972 (Montreal, Quebec)–
RECORD-BREAKING IS synonymous with the name Martin Brodeur. His long list of league and franchise records includes most career wins, most wins in a season, most regular-season shutouts, and most career shutouts but perhaps Brodeur's most cherished achievement occurred in 1997 when he scored against the Montreal Canadiens, becoming the only NHL goaltender to net a game-winning goal.

Brodeur was groomed by his father, Denis Brodeur, netminder on the 1956 bronze medal-winning Olympic team and, later, official photographer for the Canadiens.

Brodeur, who has played his entire career with New Jersey Devils, took home rookie-of-the-year honours in 1994. His distinctive hybrid form—a combination of old-style stand-up goaltending and drop-to-the-knees butterfly—requires agility, exceptional maneuverability, and a lightning glove hand. This unique combo gives Brodeur an unpredictable advantage over opposing shooters.

Brodeur led the Devils to the Stanley Cup 3 times—in 1995, 2000, and 2003—and backstopped for Canada's gold and silver World Cup teams and the spectacular 2002 Olympic gold team. He was number-one goaltender again at the 2006 Olympics and shared netminding duties for the triumphant 2010 Olympic team. This 10-time All-Star has ascended into a Gretzky-like land of records, playing in a peerless realm where he can only challenge his own standards. This future hall-of-famer's achievements may never be equaled, securing his spot as the greatest NHL goaltender of all time.

HONOURS

· Calder Trophy–1994

· Williams M. Jennings Trophy–1997, 1998, 2003, 2004

· Vezina Trophy–2003, 2004, 2007, 2008

30 Catriona Le May Doan

1970 (Saskatoon, Saskatchewan)– SPEED SKATER CATRIONA Le May Doan once said, "It's harder to be good all the time than excellent once." She surpassed her own standards, however, achieving excellence every time she set foot on the speed skating oval.

Le May Doan skated for Canada at the 1992 and 1994 Winter Olympics and, in 1996, she won the 500-metre sprint at the Worlds. She repeated that victory, and added the 1,000-metre at the following 2 World Cups. At the 1998 Nagano Olympics she captured gold in the 500-metre and bronze in the 1,000-metre. She ranked first overall in World Cup standings in both distances, dominating the long track for the next 4 years.

At the 2002 Salt Lake City Olympics, Le May Doan proudly carried the flag in the Opening Ceremonies. She soared to a world record in her gold-medal 500-metre sprint. This was an extraordinary achievement: the first time a Canadian Olympian had defended an individual gold medal. She captured the Worlds again that year, as well as the World Cup season title.

Le May Doan retired in 2003 holding the Canadian, World, and Olympic records in the 500-metre. Throughout her career she had broken world records an astonishing 13 times.

29 Lennox Lewis

1965 (London, England)– **CANADIAN-BRITISH HEAVYWEIGHT** boxer Lennox Lewis defeated the greatest names in boxing and secured Olympic gold for Canada.

Lewis immigrated to Kingston, Ontario, from England at age 12 with his mother. He played several sports in high school but with his long reach, Lewis excelled in the ring. In 1983 at age 18, Lewis won the World Junior Boxing Championship and competed for Canada at the 1984 Los Angeles Olympics.

After winning at the 1986 Commonwealth Games and the 1987 North American Championships, Lewis—a 6-time Canadian Amateur Champion—competed for Canada in the super heavyweight category at the 1988 Seoul Olympics. He needed a mere 34 seconds to defeat the reigning World Cup champion, East German Ulli Kaden, in the quarterfinals. In the gold-medal match, in a second-round technical knockout, Lewis defeated American Riddick Bowe and claimed Canada's first boxing gold medal since 1932.

With an amateur record of 85 wins and 9 losses, Lewis moved to England and turned professional. In 44 fights he recorded 41 wins (including 32 knockouts), beating such noteworthy opponents as Evander Holyfield, Mike Tyson, and Donovan Ruddock. Lewis retired in 2004 as 1 of only 3 undefeated World Heavyweight Champions.

28 Steve Podborski

1957 (Toronto, Ontario)-
STEVE PODBORSKI BROKE Europe's long dominance of downhill skiing by racing to Olympic and World Cup glory.

Podborski grew up skiing on the slopes near his home in Don Mills, Ontario, and started racing at age 13 in the local Nancy Greene League. In 1973, at the age of 16, he began touring with the Canadian National Alpine Ski Team and won a silver medal in the first race of the Can-Am Ski Series tour.

Podborski was the youngest—and winningest—member of the "Crazy Canucks" team, the group of Canadian male skiers known for their kamikaze flights down the most dangerous ski hills on the world circuit. In 1978 at Morzine, France, Podborski won his first World Cup race. Two years later at the Lake Placid Olympics he won bronze, becoming the first non-European male to win an Olympic medal.

Altogether Podborski won 8 World Cup races in the downhill event. In his stellar 1981–82 season he achieved 3 first-place and 2 second-place finishes to capture the men's World Cup downhill title for the first, and still the only time in North American history.

HONOURS

· Norton H. Crow Award–1981, 1982
· Officer of the Order of Canada–1982
· Canadian Olympic Hall of Fame–1985
· Canada's Sports Hall of Fame–1987
· Canadian Ski Hall of Fame–1988

27 Doug Harvey

1924 (Montreal, Quebec)– DOUG HARVEY—ONE of hockey's greatest defenceman and a spectacular all-round player and playmaker—joined the Montreal Canadiens in 1947. A master of pace, Harvey surveyed the ice carefully before launching a play, and controlled the game with his superlative stickhandling. He could consistently deliver blazing spot-on passes or slow the tempo to a crawl.

Harvey was quarterback for the Canadiens' famous Flying Frenchmen of the 1950s, efficiently setting up his legendary teammates Rocket Richard, Jean Béliveau, and Bernie Geoffrion. His smart set-ups were so effective on the power play that the Canadiens often scored 3 goals during a single penalty, forcing the league to change the rules to allow a penalized player to return to the ice after a goal.

Harvey played 21 seasons—14 with the Montreal Canadiens—and won 6 Stanley Cup championships. An 11-time All-Star who won 7 Norris Trophies, Harvey was traded to New York in 1960, where he led the Rangers to the playoffs as player-coach. He won the Norris Trophy again that year, making him the only player to win a major award while coaching.

26 Kurt Browning

1966 (Rocky Mountain House, Alberta)– CHAMPION FIGURE SKATER Kurt Browning, raised on a ranch in small-town Alberta, started skating at age 3 on the family's outdoor rink. He began competing at age 11 and in 1985 captured the Canadian Junior Men's title.

At the 1988 World Figure Skating Championships, 20-year-old Browning placed only 6th yet impressed the world. His performance included the first-ever successful quadruple toe-loop in competition. He returned the following year with a dazzling display of technically challenging moves including his now-trademark quadruple, a triple-triple combination, and 6 triple jumps. Browning, renowned for his exuberant footwork, won his first of 3 consecutive World Figure Skating titles—the first triple win in Canadian figure skating history.

Back injury hampered Browning's performance in the 1992 Olympics in Albertville—he finished 6th overall. Flag bearer and favourite going into the 1994 Games, Browning finished 12th after the short program, but delivered a stunning long program to finish 5th overall. Canadian fans responded to his heroic comeback by collecting gold pieces and melting them down into a medal for their beloved Browning.

This charismatic 3-time Olympian, 4-time Canadian Champion, and 4-time World Champion owns a page in the *Guinness Book of World Records* for his phenomenal quadruple toe-loop.

HONOURS

· MVP, Canada Winter Games–1991

· Esso Women's National Championships MVP–1996, 1998, 1999, 2000, 2007

· IIHF World Women's Championship MVP–1999

· Bruce Kidd Leadership Award–2000

· Olympic Winter Games MVP–2002, 2006

· Bobbie Rosenfeld Award–2007

25 Hayley Wickenheiser

1978 (Shaunavon, Saskatchewan)– A 4-TIME OLYMPIAN with a spectacular (and ongoing) 16-year career, Hayley Wickenheiser is without doubt the best female player in the history of the game. This all-seasons athlete is also an elite softball player who swung a bat for Canada at the 2000 Summer Olympics.

Dedicated and determined, with a lethal slapshot and commanding on-ice presence, Wickenheiser joined Team Canada when she was only 15 years old. In the years since, she has led her team to 6 World Championships and 11 Nations Cup gold medals. Tournament top scorer and MVP at Canada's Olympic gold-medal victories in 2002 and 2006, she was also a force in 1998's silver-medal match-up. At the 2010 Games in Vancouver, Wickenheiser proudly delivered the Athlete's Oath at the Opening Ceremonies, then went on to collect her 318th career point, and captained Canada to an inspired gold-medal triumph over the United States. Canada's all-time leader in goals, assists, games played, and penalty minutes, she also holds a record 16 goals in Olympic play.

Sports Illustrated recently ranked Wickenheiser number 20 in their Top 25 Toughest Athletes in the World, a designation she earned both for her national team performances and for holding her own while playing professional hockey in men's leagues in Finland and Sweden.

24 Gaétan Boucher

1958 (Charlesbourg, Quebec)-
A YOUNG GAÉTAN Boucher took speed skating lessons to improve his hockey skills but by age 14 was competing nationally on the oval. At his first Olympics—Montreal in 1976—he ranked 6th. By 1980 he was consistently finishing second behind the great American Eric Heiden. At Lake Placid Boucher won silver in the 1,000-metre, one of only 2 medals for Canada in those games. Boucher wasn't satisfied. He wanted gold.

Heiden retired leaving Boucher to step up. But illness and a shattered ankle left Boucher in disappointing 9th at the 1983 World Championships. Determined, he made a miraculous rebound to win several pre-Olympic events and proudly carried the flag for Canada at Sarajevo in 1984.

Boucher missed silver in the 500-metre by 2/10 of a second. He remained confident for the 1,000-metre and captured gold, breaking a long medal shut-out—a Canadian male had never won individual gold at the Winter Games. Weary with a cold, Boucher sped to a close finish in the 1,500-metre to win his second gold and the 3rd of only 4 medals for Canada at those Games, laying the foundation for what is now a Canadian sport stronghold.

HONOURS

· Canadian Olympic Hall of Fame–1984
· Lou Marsh Trophy–1984
· Norton H. Crow Award–1984
· Officer of the Order of Canada–1984
· Oscar Mathisen Award–1984

HONOURS

· Lionel Conacher Award–1984
· Officer of the Order of Canada–1984
· *Swimming World's* Male World Swimmer
  of the Year–1984
· Canadian Olympic Hall of Fame–1985

23 Alex Baumann

1964 (Prague, Czechoslovakia)-
AS EXECUTIVE DIRECTOR of Sport Canada's "Own the Podium" program in 2008, Alex Baumann declared, "We should strive to be the best in the world." This competitive spirit drove Baumann to a double-gold performance in 1984.

Baumann immigrated with his family to Sudbury, Ontario, at age 5. He began swimming competitively and by age 17 held 38 Canadian records and a world record in the 200-metre Individual Medley (IM). Over the next decade, Baumann captured 6 more world records and 34 national titles.

Injury kept Baumann out of the 1982 World Aquatic Championship, but he recovered in time to win gold in the 200- and 400-metre IM at the Commonwealth Games, more gold at the 1983 World University Games, and another world record at the 1983 Olympic trials.

Baumann was Canada's darling at the 1984 Olympics in Los Angeles, the best hope for a medal in a sport that hadn't seen Olympic gold since 1912. He didn't disappoint. His spectacular 200-metre IM earned gold and another world record; he repeated the double in the 400-metre the next day.

At the 1986 World Championship, Baumann claimed silver and bronze, followed by 3 golds at the 1986 Commonwealth Games. He retired from competitive swimming in 1987.

22 Russ Jackson

1936 (Hamilton, Ontario)-
THE MOST SUCCESSFUL Canadian-born quarterback in Canadian Football League history, Russ Jackson challenged the CFL's American-quarterback tradition to prove that a homegrown boy could make good.

Jackson was gifted in football, basketball, and academics. At the age of 22, Jackson was nominated by McMaster University for a Rhodes Scholarship, but the star quarterback chose instead to pursue a football career. He was the first-round draft pick of the Ottawa Rough Riders.

Over his 12-year career, Jackson led Ottawa to 3 Grey Cup victories. Equally talented at passing and rushing, Jackson led the CFL 5 seasons in passing (1963–67)

and maintained a 6.6-yard rushing average for a total 5,045 yards on 738 rushes—4th all-time for a CFL quarterback.

Jackson announced his retirement just prior to the 1969 Grey Cup game between Ottawa and Saskatchewan. In his final game Jackson was unstoppable, passing for 254 yards and 4 touchdowns. He was awarded game MVP—the first and last time for a Canadian-born player. Jackson, who didn't miss a game in his 12-year career, finished with 24,592 passing yards, 1,356 completions, 125 interceptions, and 185 touchdowns.

21 Percy Williams

1908 (Vancouver, British Columbia)-1982
IN THIS ERA of tall, hearty athletes, it's surprising that a diminutive runner from Vancouver performed one of the most dramatic sporting feats in Canadian history. Percy Williams, the "Canadian Cheetah" who established the 100-metre world record at the 1928 Olympics, was nearly half a metre (1.5 feet) smaller than Usain Bolt, who performed the same feat at the 2008 Games.

A sickly child, Williams had been told to avoid exercise. Instead, he took up track in high school and with lightning speed broke provincial records in the 100- and 220-yard dashes. At the 1927 Olympic trials, Williams shocked the country by tying the 100-metre Olympic record.

Williams lacked international experience and few expected him to succeed at the Amsterdam Olympics. The Canadian underdog crossed the 100-metre finish line ahead of the favoured Americans, and 3 days later captured 200-metre gold, making him the first non-American to capture double-gold sprint medals at one Olympics.

Williams was celebrated, but Americans doubted he could repeat his stunning victory. He joined the North American track circuit and demolished all doubt by winning 21 of 22 races and setting a new 100-metre world record at 10.3 seconds. Williams retired from racing in 1930.

HONOURS
· Canadian Olympic Hall of Fame—1949
· Canadian Track and Field Athlete of the Half-Century—1950
· Officer of the Order of Canada—1980

20 Marlene Stewart Streit

1934 (Cereal, Alberta)–
CANADA'S TOP FEMALE amateur golfer of all time, Marlene Stewart Streit remains the only golfer to have won the Canadian, U.S., British, and Australian amateur championships and the first Canadian to be inducted into the World Golf Hall of Fame.

Starting as a caddy at age 13, Streit won her first Canadian Ladies' Open Amateur Championship in 1951 at only 17, beating the formidable Ada Mackenzie. For the next 3 decades, Streit dominated women's golf in Canada and internationally. Between 1951 and 1977, she captured 11 Ontario titles (plus 7 second-place finishes), 11 Canadian Open titles (plus 5 second-place finishes), and 9 Canadian Closed titles. She won the British Championship at 19 and the U.S. Women's 3 years later. In 1963 she added the Australian Championship to her unmatched collection.

Although encouraged to turn professional, Streit choose to stay amateur. She represented Canada as a 5-time member of the Canadian Ladies' Golf Association (CLGA) Commonwealth team and a 7-time member of the CLGA world amateur team.

Streit's command of the fairway continued well into her senior years. She won 6 Ontario and four CLGA Senior championship titles and in 2003, at the age of 69, Streit became the oldest player to win the USGA senior championship title.

19 Fanny "Bobbie" Rosenfeld

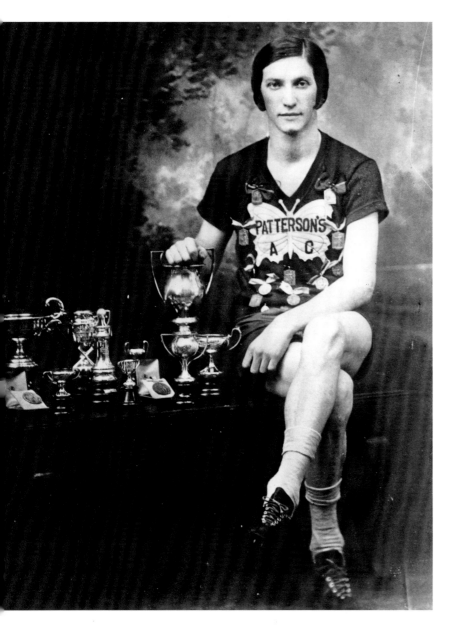

1904 (Dnepropetrovsk, Russia)–1969

TRAIL-BLAZING ALL-ROUND ATHLETE Bobbie Rosenfeld, arguably the most influential woman in Canadian sports, excelled in basketball, hockey, softball, tennis, and, most famously, as an Olympic track medalist. One writer joked, "The most efficient way to summarize Rosenfeld's career... is to say that she was not good at swimming."

Born in Russia, Rosenfeld arrived in Canada as an infant and grew up in Barrie, Ontario. She played high-level basketball and triple-A hockey, and she played shortstop for her softball club. She gained national attention in 1923 when she beat the 100-yard dash world record in a race she entered on a whim. The next year Rosenfeld won the Toronto Ladies Tennis Championship and in 1925 she dominated the Ontario Track and Field Championship, placing first in 5 different events.

At the 1928 Amsterdam Olympics Rosenfeld achieved more points than any other athlete—male or female—captured silver in the 100-metres, and won world-record gold in the 4×100-metre relay.

Severe arthritis left Rosenfeld bedridden for months in 1929. Although she continued to compete—in 1931 she was top homerun hitter in her softball league, and in 1932 she was named most outstanding female hockey player in Ontario—Rosenfeld shifted her energy to writing. Her "Sports Reel" column ran for 20 years in *The Globe and Mail*.

18 Simon Whitfield

1975 (Kingston, Ontario)–
TWO OF CANADA'S most memorable Olympic performances are Simon Whitfield's from-the-back-of-the-pack triathlon finishes in 2000 and 2008.

Triathlon became an official sport at the 2000 Sydney Olympics, and Whitfield—ranked number 1 in North America—was ready. He finished 28th in the swim, then exploded on the bike portion, moving up to 10th. Then all went awry. Whitfield and a dozen other riders crashed and, in a flash, he was 24th. He leapt back on his bike and rode like heck. He ran a thrilling road race, passing runner after runner until he caught the lead. They dueled neck-and-neck through the final kilometres until Whitfield found one final kick to claim victory and set an Olympic record.

Whitfield also captured gold at the 2001 Canadian Triathlon Championships (his second national title) and the 2002 Commonwealth Games but finished a disappointing 11th at the 2004 Olympics.

At the 2008 Olympics Whitfield repeated his come-from-behind performance. Out of medal contention going into the final kilometre yet refusing to fade, he burst into first with 200 metres to go. The German runner caught Whitfield in the final seconds, but his push for silver showed heroic strength and perseverance.

HONOURS

· Triathlon Canada Athlete of the Year—1999, 2000, 2001, 2002, 2003, 2004, 2005, 2006, 2007, 2008

17 Chantal Petitclerc

1969 (Saint-Marc-des-Carrières, Quebec)–
CHANTAL PETITCLERC DOMINATED wheelchair racing for more than 20 years and inspired millions with her determination, integrity, and competitive excellence.

Petitclerc was 13 when a barn door fell on her, crushing her spine. A trainer at university introduced her to wheelchair sports.

She competed internationally for the first time at the 1992 Paralympic Games in Barcelona, winning bronze in the 200- and 800-metres. At each successive Paralympics her medal count increased until her most remarkable performance in Athens in 2004. The unbeatable Petitclerc won 5 golds and broke 3 world records.

That year, Petitclerc refused Athletics Canada's Athlete of the Year Award because she was to share it with Olympic hurdler Perdita Felicien. Petitclerc felt that Felicien's no-medal performance was not equal to her own multiple golds, and considered the shared award a slight to Paralympic athletes.

At her final Paralympics in Beijing, Petitclerc dominated again, beating competitors 16 years her junior and claiming another 5 gold medals and setting 3 world records.

Petitclerc recognizes that she is a role model for people with disabilities but identifies herself as an athlete first. She says, "I've always seen myself as an athlete trying to go fast and win a race."

HONOURS
· Velma Springstead Award–2004, 2008
· Bobbie Rosenfeld Award–2008
· Lou Marsh Trophy–2008
· Companion of the Order of Canada–2009

HONOURS

· Velma Springstead Award–1945, 1947
· Lou Marsh Trophy–1945, 1947, 1948
· Bobbie Rosenfeld Award–1946, 1947, 1948
· Canadian Olympic Hall of Fame–1949
· Canada's Sports Hall of Fame–1955
· Officer of the Order of Canada–1991

16 Barbara Ann Scott

1928 (Ottawa, Ontario)–
IN THE YEARS following World War II, the name Barbara Ann Scott evoked visions of grace and athleticism. In a time of post-war gloom, Scott sparked national adoration, and her Olympic achievement is still unique in Canadian sport history.

Known as "Canada's Sweetheart," Scott launched her sensational career at 6, playing Raggedy Ann in an ice show. Determined and disciplined, Scott practised 8 hours a day and, at 10, was the youngest skater to pass the rigorous Gold Figures test. She won the Canadian Junior title at 11, became Canada's Senior Champion at 15, and was the first female skater to land a double lutz in competition.

In 1947, friends raised funds to send Scott to the European Championships and the Worlds. She won both. In 1948 Scott swept up, claiming Canadian, European, North American, and World championships in an exciting lead-up to the St. Moritz Olympics. She adjusted her program to suit the conditions—an outdoor rink and melting ice after two hockey games—and skated a flawless gold-medal performance.

Schools let out, bands played, and over 70,000 fans greeted Scott on her triumphant return to Ottawa. Her Olympic gold is still the only figure skating singles gold won by a Canadian skater, male or female.

15 Mario Lemieux

1965 (Montreal, Quebec)– LEGENDARY MARIO LEMIEUX is one of the finest hockey players ever and perhaps the sport's most heroic athlete.

The strapping, stellar forward broke all of Guy Lafleur's junior records before becoming the Penguins number 1 draft pick in 1984. Lemieux scored with his first shot on goal, won rookie of the year honours, and was the first rookie ever to be named All-Star MVP.

In 1988–89 Lemieux notched two 8-point games, and in 1989–90 he enjoyed a 46-game scoring streak. Despite missing 50 games in 1990–91 for back surgery, Lemieux led the Penguins to their first Stanley Cup with a phenomenal 44 playoff points—second only to Gretzky's record 47. The Penguins won again the next year, Lemieux leading the post-season scoring despite crippling back pain and missing 5 playoff games with a broken hand.

In 1993, the stalwart forward faced a diagnosis of life-threatening Hodgkin's Lymphoma. He endured energy-sapping treatments, yet returned to lead the Penguins on a record 17-game winning streak.

Lemieux retired in 1996 and bought the bankrupt Penguins. The 3-time Hart Trophy winner and 6-time NHL scoring leader came out of retirement in 2000 as player–owner and notched 76 points in only 43 games. Lemieux retired for the final time in 2006. With the Penguins 2009 Stanley Cup triumph, "Super Mario" is the only person to capture the Cup as both player and owner.

14 Nancy Greene

1943 (Ottawa, Ontario)-
IT'S BEEN 40 years since fresh-faced "Tiger" soared to Olympic gold, but Nancy Greene is still the best-known name in Canadian skiing. In the 1960s Greene captured a record number of Canadian and World titles, along with the hearts of Canadians.

Greene, who grew up in mountainous Rossland, B.C., was racing at age 13 and won her first trophy in 1958 at 15—coming second to her sister in the Canadian Junior Championship. Sibling rivalry prodded Greene to improve enough to make the 1960 Olympic Team.

Nicknamed "Tiger" because of her aggressive skiing style, this 3-time Olympian raced to 7 Canadian Champion titles, 3 U.S. Champion titles, and 13 World Cup victories—still a record for a Canadian competitor. For her World Cup title in 1967, Greene won by a scant 0.07 seconds in the final race of the season.

At the 1968 Grenoble Olympics, 24-year-old Greene—skiing with an injured ankle—won silver in the slalom and then blasted down the giant slalom course to capture the gold by a margin of 2.68 seconds—one of the most decisive wins in Olympic history.

Canada's beloved "Ski Queen" returned to ticker-tape parades and country-wide celebrations—one of the greatest outpourings of jubilation in Canadian sports history.

HONOURS

· Bobbie Rosenfeld Award–1967, 1968
· Velma Springstead Award–1967, 1968
· Lou Marsh Trophy–1967, 1968
· Canada's Sports Halls of Fame–1967
· Officer of the Order of Canada–1968
· Canadian Olympic Hall of Fame–1971
· CP Female Athlete of the Century–1999

HONOURS

· Canadian Olympic Hall of Fame–1994
· Wilson and McCall Trophy (with Kathleen Heddle)–1995, 1996
· Canada's Sports Hall of Fame–1997
· Thomas Keller Medal–2002

13 Marnie McBean

1968 (Vancouver, British Columbia)- MARNIE MCBEAN'S VERSATILITY is unmatched in women's rowing. Individually, she became the first woman rower to claim a medal in every boat class at World and Olympic events, and with partner Kathleen Heddle, she became the most decorated Summer Olympian in Canadian history.

McBean captured her first medal—a bronze—at the 1986 World Junior Championships. In 1991, pairing with Heddle, McBean won gold and set a world record at the World Championships. The terrific twosome captured Olympic gold at the 1992 Olympics in Barcelona, as well as a second gold as part of the women's eight.

In 1995 McBean persuaded Heddle out of retirement to compete at the Atlanta Olympics. The duo captured gold in doubles scull and added a bronze in quad.

McBean took up single-scull racing in 1993 and again rose to world-champion level. After winning silver at the World Championships—finishing second to teammate Silken Laumann—McBean captured 3 World Cup, 8 U.S., and 3 Canadian titles, as well as a gold medal at the 1999 Pan American Games.

McBean had hoped for a singles medal to add to her Olympic collection, but was forced by injury to withdraw 3 weeks before the Sydney Games in 2000.

HONOURS

· Canadian Professional Golf Tour Rookie
  of the Year–1993
· Lionel Conacher Award–2000, 2001, 2003
· Lou Marsh Trophy–2003
· Member of the Order of Canada–2009
· Canadian Golf Hall of Fame–2009

12 Mike Weir

1970 (Sarnia, Ontario)–
WORLD-CHAMPION GOLFER Mike Weir developed his impressive swing at Huron Oaks Golf Course in Sarnia. After winning the 1988 Ontario Junior Championship and placing second in the 1991 and 1992 Canadian Amateur Championships, the talented golfer turned professional.

In 1999 Weir won his first PGA Tour title on Canadian soil—the first Canadian to do so since 1954. The next year, 30-year-old Weir became the first Canadian to play in the President's Cup. He topped the season at the World Golf Championship in Spain by defeating an overwhelming field that included Tiger Woods, Vijay Singh, and Lee Westwood.

2003 was a stellar year for Weir. Canadians collectively held their breath as he defeated Len Mattiace on the first extra hole and became the first Canadian to win the prestigious Masters Tournament. Two months later, Weir ranked 3rd in the U.S. Open and finished the year ranked 3rd in Official World Golf Rankings.

In the 2007 Presidents Cup, Weir was matched in the singles competition against the incomparable Tiger Woods. Weir emerged victorious from the emotionally charged duel.

Still active in the professional tour, Weir has matched and may even pass George Knudson's record of 8 PGA Tour wins by a Canadian.

11 Maurice "Rocket" Richard

1921 (Montreal, Quebec)–2000
MAURICE "ROCKET" RICHARD'S state funeral—the only one ever held for a Canadian athlete—revealed the unique place the Montreal Canadiens hero held in the hearts of hockey fans and the people of Quebec.

Richard, who learned to play hockey in a rough, working-class district of Montreal, joined the Canadiens in 1942. The intensely driven right-winger earned his nickname for his explosive flights across the blueline, deking opponents, intense eyes blazing like the flare of a rocket. In his 18-year career, Richard took the Canadiens to 8 Stanley Cups, led the league in goals for 5 years, was the first to score 500 goals, and retired as

the all-time scoring leader with 544 goals. His record for most points in one game (8) stood until 1976, and his 1944–45 record 50-goals-in-50-games was on the books until 1981.

Richard's legendary temper caused one of the most notorious events in NHL history. On March 15, 1955, Richard punched a linesman and was suspended for the remainder of the season and the playoffs. Enraged Montreal fans rioted in the streets, and Richard appealed for peace on Quebec radio.

No other athlete has provoked such fierce loyalty and respect as the tough, gifted Rocket from Montreal.

10 Clara Hughes

1972 (Winnipeg, Manitoba)– SIX-TIME OLYMPIC medalist Clara Hughes is unique in the annals of Canadian sport. Her determination, athleticism, and competitive focus made her a world-class athlete in two diverse sports. Hughes became fascinated with speed skating as a teenager while watching the 1988 Calgary Olympics. Although she embraced the sport, it wasn't on the oval that Hughes first made her mark, but on the bicycle track as one of Canada's best-ever cyclists.

Hughes's cycling career includes international and national titles; she has been Canadian Cycling champion a record 18 times, and won double bronze at the 1996 Summer Olympics—one in the individual road race and the other for individual time trial. In one of her most memorable accomplishments, Hughes—respected for her explosive power—wore the coveted yellow jersey for 4 days during the grueling Tour de France road race in 1994.

Hughes finished her cycling career at the top, winning gold and bronze at the 2002 Commonwealth Games, and gold and silver at the 2003 Pan American Games.

In 2000, after a 10-year break from the ice, Hughes returned to speed skating. In an unprecedented display of athletic determination, Hughes was selected for the national team after only 7 weeks of training. Two years later, she thrilled the sporting world by capturing bronze in the exhausting 5,000-metre event at the 2002 Olympics.

The world's top long-distancer, Hughes achieved World Cup gold in the 3,000-metres in 2002 and 2004, 5,000-metre gold in 2005, and World Championship 5,000-metre gold in 2004—a Canadian first. At the same event, she notched a World Record in the 10,000-metre event. At the 2006 Turin Olympics, Hughes—in a dramatic come-from-behind victory—clinched gold in the 5,000-metres, followed by a team-pursuit silver.

Hughes—the only athlete in the world to win multiple medals in both Summer and Winter Olympics—was chosen as Canada's flag bearer for the 2010 Vancouver Games. She thrilled the Canadian crowd by winning a bronze medal in the 5,000-metre event with track-record speed. This remarkable achievement elevated Hughes to legendary status in Canadian sports. With her six medals she joined teammate Cindy Klassen as the most decorated Olympian in Canadian history.

HONOURS

· Tip O'Neill Award–1987, 1990, 1992, 1994,
  1995, 1997, 1998, 2001, 2002
· Gold Glove Award–1992, 1993, 1997, 1998,
  1999, 2001, 2002
· Silver Slugger Award–1992, 1997, 1999
· National League MVP–1997
· Lionel Conacher Award–1998
· Lou Marsh Trophy–1998
· Canada's Sports Hall of Fame–2007
· Canadian Baseball Hall of Fame–2009

9 Larry Walker

1966 (Maple Ridge, British Columbia)-
LARRY WALKER ACHIEVED the greatest stats
of any Canadian player in Major League
Baseball: most games played (1,988), hits
(2,160), homeruns (383), runs scored (1,355),
RBIS (1,311—passed in 2006 by Justin
Morneau, and stolen bases (230).

Like most hockey-mad Canadian boys,
Walker grew up dreaming of playing in the
NHL, and apparently had the goaltending
chops to get there. "I don't mind saying
hockey is the greatest game in the world," he
admitted. But Walker's father coached him
and his 3 older brothers on one of the best
softball teams in Canada.

The Montreal Expos scouted Walker
while he was playing on the Canadian
National Junior Team; they signed the
18-year-old in 1984 and he played his first
professional game in 1989. Walker became
a National League All-Star within 2 years.

The stellar right-fielder and outstanding
hitter was leading the Expos to an almost
certain World Series in 1994 when the infamous Major League strike occurred. The
season never resumed, and the next year
Walker signed with the expansion Colorado
Rockies. He flourished with the Rockies and
in 1997 was the National League's MVP with
career highs of 153 games, 568 at bats, 49
homeruns—the NL lead for that year—and
130 RBIS.

Walker—a 3-time National League bat-
ting champion (1998, 1999, 2001)—orches-
trated a trade to the St. Louis Cardinals in
2004, hoping for a run at the World Series.
They made it to the finals, but the Boston
Red Sox swept the series and denied Walker's chance for the title.

Walker, a proud Canadian with a Maple
Leaf tattooed on his arm, retired at the end
of the 2005 season. Despite being plagued
by injury throughout his 17-year career—he
never played an entire 162-game season—
Walker accumulated a long list of outstanding accomplishments. Along with the MVP
honours, his accolades include 5 All-Star
selections, 7 Gold Gloves for excellence in
the outfield, 3 Silver Slugger Awards, and
an unprecedented 9 Tip O'Neill Awards as
Canada's baseball player of the year. At the
ceremony to induct Walker into the Canadian Baseball Hall of Fame, Tom Valcke,
President of the Hall, exclaimed, "There's no
question he's the greatest Canadian ever to
put a bat in his hands."

8 Ferguson "Fergie" Jenkins

1943 (Chatham, Ontario)–
THE GREATEST HONOUR for professional baseball players is membership in the exclusive Baseball Hall of Fame in Cooperstown, New York. Only one Canadian has been given that honour—the great Ferguson Jenkins. One of the finest pitchers in Major League Baseball, Jenkins' control and pinpoint accuracy was legendary.

Young Jenkins was an all-round athlete who played Junior B hockey and basketball for the Harlem Globetrotters during baseball's off-season. In 1962 the Philadelphia Phillies drafted Jenkins straight out of high school. Yet it wasn't until he was traded to the Chicago Cubs in 1966 that Jenkins truly came into his own as a starting pitcher.

Jenkins was an imposing powerhouse with a hard and deadly accurate throw. He finished the 1967 season with 20 wins, an earned run average of 2.80, a league-high 20 complete games, a Cubs record 236 strikeouts, and an appearance in the All-Star Game. He finished an impressive second in Cy Young Award balloting.

Jenkins dominated the pitcher's mound for the next 6 years, winning 20 or more games each season. In 1969 he led the National League in strikeouts with 273. In 1971—with a league-high 24 wins and 325 innings, and pitching 30 complete games—he became the first Cub and first Canadian to win the Cy Young Award. This was even more impressive given that he pitched at Wrigley Field, the most hitter-friendly ballpark in the Major Leagues.

In 1971 Jenkins, also a decent hitter, broke the Cubs club record for homeruns (6) and RBIS (20) by a pitcher, and had a respectable 13 career-homerun record.

He was traded to the Texas Rangers in 1973 and still holds that team's season records for most wins (25), shutouts (6), and complete games (29), all achieved in 1974. He was traded to the Boston Red Sox in 1975, returned to the Rangers in 1977, and went back to the Cubs in 1982. He retired in 1983.

Jenkins's precise pitching produced 284 wins over his 19 years in the Majors. He holds one of the highest strikeout records (3,192) and is the only member of the elite 3,000-strikeout club to finish his career with less than 1,000 walks. The 1991 Major League Baseball All-Star Game held in Toronto was dedicated to Jenkins, who threw the ceremonial first pitch.

7 Gordie Howe

1928 (Floral, Saskatchewan)–
GRETZKY MAY BE "The Great One," but there is only one "Mr. Hockey." Gordie Howe—powerful forward, terrific scorer, and the most admired and feared player during his phenomenal decades-long career—led his Detroit Red Wings to 4 Stanley Cups. With 1,071 career goals and 2,589 career points, Howe will always be one of the most notable athletes in Canadian sports history.

Born in a farmhouse near Floral, Saskatchewan just before the Great Depression, Howe grew up playing hockey in the intensely cold prairie winters. Out of this tough background grew a tall, exceptionally powerful and athletic player.

Eighteen-year-old Howe made his professional debut with the Detroit Red Wings in 1946. Fans and players were awed by Howe's supreme all-round abilities—a unique combination of ultra-smooth skating, hard-hitting corner play, and an ambidextrous ability to both stickhandle and shoot accurately on either side.

Howe won the NHL MVP and leading-scorer awards 6 times each; played in 21 NHL All-Star games; finished in the top 5 in NHL scoring for an amazing 20 straight seasons; and passed Maurice Richard's all-time points record in 1960—a record he then held for 29 years.

Howe's stamina is legendary. Not only did he play for over 3 decades—26 years in the NHL and 6 in the WHA, with a record for the most regular-season NHL games at 1,767—he adapted brilliantly to each era's style of play. And Howe spent much of this time actually on the ice. He often played a full 45 minutes when the average was only 25 and, in 1979—his final season at age 51—he completed a full 80-game season.

Howe was respected by other players for his stickhandling and shooting abilities and feared for his physical game. The hard-hitting forward left his mark on many opponents, and tales of encounters in the corner with Howe are legendary. As a rookie in his first game in Montreal, Howe famously knocked out cold the tough Rocket Richard with one punch. An unofficial NHL achievement commemorates Howe's magical combination of skills—a "Gordie Howe Hat Trick" marks a goal, an assist, and a fight in a single game.

Howe retired for good in 1980, but made one more professional appearance in 1997 at—believe it!—70 years old. He still—and probably forever—holds the record for career regular-season goals–975 (WHA and NHL combined).

6 Donovan Bailey

1967 (Manchester, Jamaica)- TRADITION STATES THAT the holder of the world record in the men's 100-metre sprint is crowned Fastest Man in the World. A Canadian has legitimately achieved this honour only twice in history (Ben Johnson's mark was removed from the record book). The first was Percy Williams in 1928. The second, almost 70 years later, was Donovan Bailey in one of the most competitive, pressure-filled 100-metre finals in Olympic history.

Bailey—who immigrated to Oakville, Ontario, at age 13—was a speedy kid and fierce competitor in all sports. Young Bailey's passion, however, was more for basketball than track. It wasn't until he watched the 1990 Canadian Track and Field Championships that it dawned on him how exceptional his speed might be—he had beaten several of the national team members before. His competitive spirit kicked in and he got serious about sprinting.

Legendary track coach Don Pfaff watched Bailey compete and recognized his potential. Bailey trained intensively under Pfaff and began competing—and winning— at world-class events. He won 100-metre gold at the 1995 World Championships, and in early 1996 broke the 50-metre world record with a time of 5.56—a mark that still stands.

Bailey was the favourite going into the 1996 Atlanta Olympics. Along with this pressure, Bailey carried the extra burden of competing in Ben Johnson's shadow. Canadians longed to dispel the shame of Johnson's fall from grace, and Bailey was their hope. If this wasn't enough stress, the 100-metre final began with 3 false starts and a disqualification. The pressure would have thrown many athletes, but Bailey thrived under the added tension. The intensely focused Bailey—a warrior-sprinter with long powerful legs—accelerated from behind to capture the gold in world-record time—9.84 seconds. Even better for Canadian fans, this victory took place on American soil in a sport dominated for decades by American athletes. Bailey won his second Olympic gold only days later, anchoring the 4×100-metre relay team.

Bailey was the undisputed Fastest Man in the World in all eyes except those of Michael Johnson, the American 200-metre world champion. Johnson promoted himself after the Olympics as "the world's fastest man," and although Bailey initially ignored his challenge, they eventually competed in a one-on-one 150-metre challenge at Toronto's SkyDome in 1998. Bailey triumphantly took home the $1.5 million prize.

HONOURS

· CP Male Athlete of the Half-Century–1950
· Canada's Sports Hall of Fame–1955
· Canadian Football Hall of Fame–1963
· Canadian Lacrosse Hall of Fame–1966
· Hockey Hall of Fame–1994
· The Lionel Conacher Award is presented to
  Canada's male athlete of the year

5 Lionel Conacher

1900 (Toronto, Ontario)–1954

LIONEL "BIG TRAIN" Conacher epitomized the term "all-round athlete." Driven and determined, he excelled in team sports such as football, lacrosse, and hockey as well as the individual ones of boxing and wrestling. One of 10 children, Conacher quit school after grade 8 and turned to sports as a way to support his family. At 12 he played rugby with the Toronto Capitals, and over the next 8 years he contributed to 14 different teams, including an astonishing 11 championship teams.

Ontario Amateur Lightweight Wrestling champ at age 16, 4 years later Conacher owned the 1920 National Light Heavyweight boxing title. His phenomenal speed and power meant that he was a natural on the gridiron—he led the Toronto Argonauts to Grey Cup victory in 1921, scoring 15 of their 23 points.

When Conacher switched to hockey, it seemed he was destined to be on ice. He'd only started skating at age 16 but was drawn to the higher salaries and faster play of hockey. A cunning defenceman, he charged into the NHL, carrying the Chicago Black Hawks to a Stanley Cup in 1934. In 1935, he captained the Cup-winning Montreal Maroons to victory. Some say hockey was his weakest sport.

Amazingly, Conacher was one of Canada's most skilled lacrosse players and an extraordinary baseballer. One particular day in 1921 is legendary: he led the Toronto Hillcrests to victory by slamming a game-winning double in the last inning. He then raced across town to join the Toronto Maitlands on the lacrosse field, where his team was down 2–1 and scored 2 goals to secure victory.

Conacher earned the affectionate "Big Train" moniker for his dominating presence on whichever field he chose to play, and he was named Canada's Outstanding Athlete of the Half-Century for his enduring success in a range of athletic endeavours.

Lionel Conacher retired from professional sports in 1937 at age 37, the most respected and beloved athlete in the country. He died at only 54 years old, appropriately in the middle of a baseball game. The "Big Train" suffered a heart attack on the field after running out a spectacular triple.

In an era when playing multiple sports was encouraged, no one could match Conacher's phenomenal achievements.

4 Cindy Klassen

1979 (Winnipeg, Manitoba)–
WORLD RECORD HOLDER over several distances and 4-time World Champion, speed skater Cindy Klassen has been adorned with a phenomenal 6 Olympic medals, sharing the honour with Clara Hughes for most decorated Olympian in Canadian history.

Klassen began skating in 1981, at age 2, but her passion for speed skating was a late discovery. The all-round athlete competed at a national level in field lacrosse, in-line skating, and hockey before focusing on the oval. A champion from her first race in 1998, Klassen won the Junior World Speed Skating Championship title in 1999 and captured her first Olympic medal—bronze in the 3,000 metres—at Salt Lake in 2002.

The next year was stellar for Klassen. At the 2003 World Sprint Championships, she finished second overall; a month later she claimed the overall title at the World All-round Speed Skating Championships (best over 4 distances: 500, 1,500, 3,000, and 5,000 metres). For the first time in 15 years one skater captured overall medals at both events, and Klassen was the first Canadian in 27 years to win a world overall title. To cap this remarkable year, she captured the 1,500-metre World Cup Title.

Despite missing the entire following season due to injury (she collided with the blade of another skater and severed 12 tendons in her right arm), Klassen stormed back in 2005 to win the 1,500-metre World Cup Title and 2 World Championship golds in the 1,500-metre and 3000-metre.

Klassen entered the 2006 Turin Olympics as the world's top contender and finished the Games as Canada's Olympic star. She won a startling 5 medals: 2 bronze

HONOURS

· Bobbie Rosenfeld Award–2005, 2006
· Velma Springstead Award–2005, 2006
· Lou Marsh Trophy–2006
· Oscar Mathisen Award–2006

(5,000– and 3,000-metre), 2 silver (1,000-metre and team pursuit), and gold (1,500-metre). Klassen is the first Canadian to win 5 medals at a single Olympics. Add in her bronze from 2002 and she became the exalted holder of the most Olympic medals in Canadian history. Klassen was a natural pick for flag bearer at the Closing Ceremonies.

Later in 2006, Klassen again captured the Overall World Cup title in the 3,000 and World Allround Championship with firsts in all 4 distances. Injuries kept her off the oval for the next few seasons, but in December 2009 she was included in *Sports Illustrated*'s list of the Top 10 Olympian Women of the Decade. While she didn't reach the podium, Klassen was a strong competitor at the 2010 Vancouver Games.

3 Steve Nash

1974 (Johannesburg, South Africa)- STEVE NASH, THE pride of Victoria, B.C., is without question the most outstanding basketball player Canada has ever produced. By age 13, this 2-time NBA MVP understood that basketball was his destiny.

The 1992 B.C. high school player of the year was picked up by California's Santa Clara University, where he changed the fortunes of the flailing college team. In his 3rd year, Nash was Conference Player of the Year and league leader in points and assists. He repeated his Conference leading performance the next year, and leapt onto the radar of NBA scouts and coaches.

The Phoenix Suns selected Nash in the first round of the 1996 entry draft. After 3 unremarkable seasons he was traded to Dallas, where he made his mark. An outstanding ball-handler, playmaker, and passer, Nash notched 7.9 points per game in his first season as a Maverick, and 8.6 points in the following year. In his spectacular 2000–01 season he averaged 15.6 points and 7.3 assists per game, pushing the Mavericks to the Western Conference Semifinals for the first time in 10 years. Next year's numbers—17.9 points and 7.7 assists—drove Nash to the All-Star Game and another playoff run. He matched those averages in 2002–03 but this time led the Mavs to the Conference Finals, where they lost to league champs San Antonio Spurs.

Nash's numbers dipped the following year, prompting a trade. The Suns were eager to have Nash back, and he proved them prescient. In one season under Nash's leadership, the Suns went from losing to being the winningest team in the league.

HONOURS

- Lionel Conacher Award–2002, 2005, 2006
- Lou Marsh Trophy–2005
- Dr. James Naismith Award–2005
- NBA MVP–2005, 2006
- J. Walter Kennedy Citizenship Award–2007
- Officer of the Order of Canada–2007

Nash recorded career-high points (18.8), rebounds (4.2), field goal percentage (.512), and free-throw percentage (a league-leading .921), and led the league with 10.5 assists per game. At the end of the 2005 season, Nash became the first Canadian and only 3rd point guard to receive the NBA MVP Award.

Nash repeated the phenomenal MVP feat in 2006, directing his team to a division title and league high-score honours, and narrowly missed a third MVP honour in 2007.

While his play has evened out in seasons since, Nash has consistently played at a high level. At the end of the 2008–09 season, his 90 percent free-throw average was second best in NBA history, and his career 3-point average (43.2 percent) was 5th. Nash was starting point guard for the 2010 NBA All-Star Game. This 7-time NBA All-Star has raised the profile of basketball in Canada and dared young Canadian basketballers to dream.

HONOURS

- Calder Trophy–1967
- James Norris Trophy–1968, 1969, 1970, 1971, 1972, 1973, 1974, 1975
- Art Ross Trophy–1970, 1975
- Conn Smythe Trophy–1970, 1972
- Hart Trophy–1970, 1971, 1972
- Lionel Conacher Award–1970
- Lou Marsh Trophy–1970

- *Sports Illustrated* Sportsman of the Year–1970
- Lester B. Pearson Award–1975
- Lester Patrick Trophy–1979
- Hockey Hall of Fame–1979
- Officer of the Order of Canada–1979
- Canada's Sports Hall of Fame–1982 (Team Canada), 2005
- Number 4 retired by Boston Bruins

2 Bobby Orr

1948 (Parry Sound, Ontario)–
THE NAME BOBBY ORR evokes both awe and heartbreak. The greatest defenceman and most well-rounded player in hockey history, Orr played only 9 full seasons in the NHL. Recurring knee injuries forced him to retire early, but Orr's extraordinary abilities provoke one of the greatest hockey what-ifs: what if he had played out a full career?

The great blueliner started out a pint-sized but speedy hockey prodigy. Orr's father recognized the enormous talent of his small son and arranged intensive coaching. Orr progressed rapidly and at 12 was noticed by the Boston Bruins, who signed him to a junior contract. They arranged for him to play with the Junior A Oshawa Generals at age 14 against players as old as 20. At 17, Orr averaged 2 points per game as he led the Generals to the OHA championship.

By 18, undersized Orr had grown into a strapping man with unmatched abilities. Alan Eagleson negotiated Orr's first contract with the Bruins in 1966, making him the highest-paid player in NHL history and ushering in the era of the agent.

In his first NHL game—against the Detroit Red Wings and the great Gordie Howe—Orr scored his first assist and impressed the crowd with his defensive

versatility: blocking shots, keeping forwards from the net, and delivering well-timed checks. At season's end Orr captured the rookie-of-the-year award.

In his most spectacular season (1969–70), Orr amassed 120 points (33 goals, 87 assists) to secure the NHL scoring title. He led the Bruins to their first Stanley Cup in 29 years with his famous Cup-clinching overtime goal against St. Louis (captured in one of the most famous hockey photos). Orr won 4 major awards that season: the Hart, Norris, Art Ross, and Conn Smythe trophies—the only player to have done so.

Orr's six 100-plus-point seasons peaked in 1974–75 with a phenomenal 135 points (46 goals, 89 assists) that topped the league. Orr is still the only defender in NHL history to have led the league in scoring. The NHL plus-minus leader for six years, his +124 rating in 1970 still stands as the highest ever for a single season.

Orr retired in 1979—after countless surgeries, his ravaged knees wouldn't last another season. He was inducted into the Hockey Hall of Fame that year, the youngest inductee ever at only 31 years. "What if," indeed.

· Lou Kaplan Trophy–1979

· Hart Trophy–1980, 1981, 1982, 1983, 1984,
  1985, 1986, 1987, 1989

· Lady Byng Trophy–1980, 1991, 1992, 1994, 1999

· Lionel Conacher Award–1980, 1981, 1982,
  1983, 1985, 1989

· Art Ross Trophy–1981, 1982, 1983, 1984, 1985,
  1986, 1987, 1990, 1991, 1994

· *Sports Illustrated* Sportsman of the Year–1982

· Lester B. Pearson Award–1982, 1983, 1984, 1985, 1987

· Lou Marsh Trophy–1982, 1983, 1985, 1989

· Conn Smythe Trophy–1985, 1988

· Lester Patrick Trophy–1994

· Canada's Sports Hall of Fame–1999

· CP and Broadcast News Association Male Athlete
  of the Century–1999

· International Ice Hockey Hall of Fame–2000

· Companion of the Order of Canada–2009

· Number 99 retired by the NHL

1 Wayne Gretzky:
THE GREAT ONE

1961 (Brantford, Ontario)- WAYNE GRETZKY, THE greatest Canadian athlete of all time—the skinny, blond forward with the brilliant smile—delighted sports fans for 2 decades as he dominated the NHL with his calm manner and supernatural talent, toppling record after record.

It's a classic Canadian story: A boy from small-town Ontario learns to play hockey on an improvised frozen rink in his backyard. He practises for hours upon hours, takes to heart his father's words—"skate to where the puck is going, not to where it's been"—and is soon outplaying boys twice his age and size. At 15 he's playing in the OHL and at 16 is the youngest player ever to lead the World Junior Championship in scoring. At 17 he's in the WHA and thrilled to play in an All-Star game with his hero, the great Gordie Howe. Young Gretzky wanted number 9 in honour of his idol, but of course it's taken; he settles for the soon-to-be-famous 99. By 1979 the wonder kid is playing in the NHL with the Edmonton Oilers, and the dynasty begins. In his rookie year, the 18-year-old scores a remarkable 137 points to tie the league lead for scoring.

Gretzky's uncanny ability to anticipate the play—to always appear in the right spot in time to make the most intelligent move—sent him soaring past the records of hockey's most legendary players, and at an absurdly young age. At only 20, Gretzky broke 2 of hockey's most impressive season marks: Bobby Orr's for assists and Phil Esposito's for points. His next record may

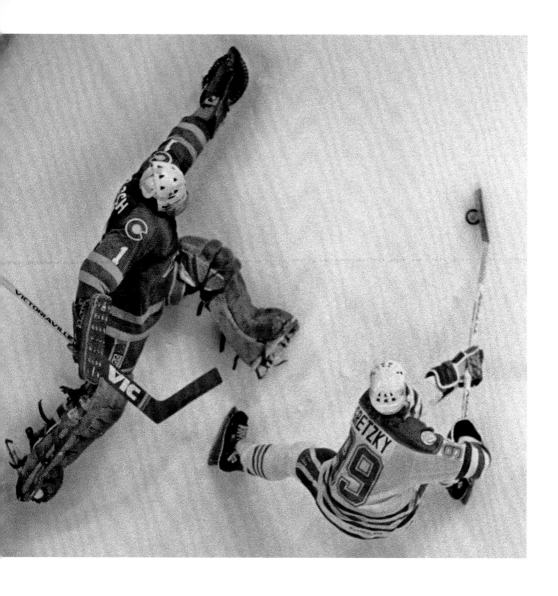

never be broken—the magical 50-goals in just 39 games. In 1983–84, he launched a 51-game point-scoring streak during which he averaged exactly 3 points per game, scoring 61 goals and 92 assists for 153 points, the first of 2 times he hit the record for most goals in a 50-game period.

Gretzky led the Edmonton Oilers to 4 Stanley Cups and proudly directed Canada to 3 Canada Cup victories. When he retired in 1999, Gretzky held a staggering 61 records, which is a record in itself. His regular-season records include most goals (92), assists (163), and points (215) in a season.

Gretzky holds the NHL record for most career regular season goals (894), assists

(1,963), and hat tricks (50). His 2,857 all-time points record appears unbreakable with the next-closest player, his old teammate Mark Messier, at a still-impressive 1,887. Gretzky's career total for assists is greater than any other player's total points. He passed his hero Gordie Howe's 26-year career point total (1,850) in only 10 years and finished with an astounding career point total of 3,239.

Gretzky was traded from Edmonton to the Los Angeles Kings in 1988, where he created a hockey frenzy like the 22-year-old franchise had never known. Hockey royalty had come to town, and the stars of L.A.— actors, musicians, politicians, and other

athletes—took notice, lining up for rink-side seats. Eight years later Gretzky donned a St. Louis Blues jersey, then went to the New York Rangers, where he played out the final years of his incomparable hockey career.

Gretzky took home the NHL's MVP award an amazing 9 times (8 consecutively)—more than any other athlete has won an MVP award in the history of major league sport. Gretzky played his final NHL game on April 18, 1999. The NHL retired number 99 across the league; baseball's Jackie Robinson is the only other professional athlete to share this honour.

In 2010, Gretzky—The Great One, Canada's greatest athlete of all time—was the final torchbearer and (with Nancy Greene, Steve Nash, Catriona Le May Doan, and Rick Hansen) lit the cauldron at the Opening Ceremonies of the Vancouver Winter Olympics.

SPECIAL HONOUR
Terry Fox

1958 (Winnipeg, Manitoba)–1981
AND THEN THERE is Terry.

For Canadians and millions of other people around the world, Terry Fox is in a category all his own—Canada's single greatest athlete and hero. For schoolchildren too young to have witnessed his extraordinary feat, Fox is a folk hero whose story they know by heart—his diagnosis of cancer, his loss of a leg, his determination to ease the suffering of others with cancer, his 5,342-kilometre Marathon of Hope that began in 1980 with the iconic image of Fox dipping his prosthetic leg in the Atlantic Ocean. It ended with his tragic death on June 28, 1982, but his spectacular achievement lives on in the annual fundraising events that bear his name.

The curly-headed boy from Port Coquitlam, B.C., played several sports growing up but was most passionate about basketball. But there was a problem: Fox was short and slight and—worst of all—a terrible player. Stubborn and determined, he practised every free moment and improved enough to earn the starting guard position on his high school team and the Athlete of the Year award. His persistence led to a spot on Simon Fraser University's varsity team.

This same mental toughness and resolve helped Terry push through his cancer diagnosis and the devastating loss of his leg, and enabled him to stick to the rigorous training program necessary for his epic odyssey across Canada. The courageous 21-year-old pushed himself until he was able to run an

astonishing average of 40 kilometres a day—the equivalent of a daily marathon. And he kept it up for 143 days. And on only one good leg.

No one before had accomplished such a gruelling, athletic feat. And Terry's legacy is both global—over $400 million has been raised worldwide for cancer research—and personal. A 6-year-old boy named Steve Nash rose early each morning in the spring of 1980 to watch Terry run. "He was a big influence," Nash said about his childhood hero. "I'm not sure there are many stories like [his] around the world. Who grew up and had someone enter their lives like that, who came from nowhere to become a national hero all for the right reasons and motives?"

Persistence, determination, and courage—something seen in the greatest of Canada's athletes—are traits Terry had in spades. And each year, on Terry Fox Day, Canadians are given the opportunity to relive the story of Canada's finest.

ABBREVIATIONS

AHL	American Hockey League
AL	American League (MLB)
CAAWS	Canadian Association for the Advancement of Women and Sport
CFL	Canadian Football League
CPGA	Canadian Professional Golf Association
CLGA	Canadian Ladies Golf Association
COC	Canadian Olympic Committee
COSIDA	College Sports Information Directors of America
CP	Canadian Press
CSHOF	Canada's Sports Hall of Fame
FIFA	International Football Association (soccer)
FIS	International Ski Federation
FISA	International Rowing Federation
HHOF	Hockey Hall of Fame
IIHF	International Ice Hockey Federation
IOF	International Olympic Committee
LPGA	Ladies Professional Golf Association
MLB	Major League Baseball
MVP	Most Valuable Player
NBA	National Basketball Association
NFL	National Football League
NHA	National Hockey Association
NHL	National Hockey League
NHLPA	National Hockey League Players Association
NL	National League (MLB)
NLL	National Lacrosse League
NSCAA	National Soccer Coaches Association of America
PCHA	Pacific Coast Hockey Association
PGA	Professional Golf Association
RBI	in MLB, runs batted in
RCGA	Royal Canadian Golf Association
USGA	United States Golf Association
USL W-League	United Soccer League's professional women's division
WCC	West Coast Conference (U.S. College)
WCHL	Western Canada Hockey League
WHA	World Hockey Association

AWARDS

Art Ross Trophy—NHL player who leads the league in points at the end of the season

Avelino Gomez Memorial Award—Canadian jockey who has made significant contributions to the sport

Bill Masterton Memorial Trophy—NHL player who best exemplifies the qualities of perseverance, sportsmanship, and dedication to hockey, as selected by the Professional Hockey Writers' Association

Bobbie Rosenfeld Award—Canada's female athlete of the year, as selected by members of the Canadian Press

Bruce Kidd Leadership Award—a national team athlete who has provided meaningful contributions to sport as a leader, advocate, change agent, or builder, presented by the Spirit of Sport Foundation

Calder Memorial Trophy—NHL's outstanding rookie, as selected by the Professional Hockey Writers' Association

Conn Smythe Trophy—MVP in the Stanley Cup playoffs, as selected by the Professional Hockey Writers' Association

Cy Young Award—MLB's best pitcher (one in the American League, one in the National League), as selected by the Baseball Writers Association of America

Dick Suderman Award—CFL's MVP in the Grey Cup game, as selected by the Football Reporters of Canada

Eddie James Memorial Trophy—CFL's leading rusher in the West Division, as selected by the Football Reporters of Canada

Frank J. Selke Trophy—NHL forward who demonstrates the most skill in the defensive component of the game, as selected by the Professional Hockey Writers' Association

George Woolf Memorial Jockey Award—thoroughbred jockey who demonstrates high standards of personal and professional conduct, on and off the racetrack, as selected by the Jockey's Guild

Gold Glove Award—MLB player who demonstrates superior individual fielding performance, as selected by manager and coaches

Hart Memorial Trophy—NHL player who is the most valuable to his team, as selected by Professional Hockey Writers' Association

Honda-Broderick Cup-outstanding collegiate woman athlete of the year (U.S.) as selected by a national panel of more than 1000 U.S. collegiate athletic directors

J. Walter Kennedy Citizenship Award—NBA player who shows outstanding dedication and service to the community, as selected by the Professional Basketball Writers' Association

Dr. James Naismith Award of Excellence—Canadian basketball player who has significantly enhanced the Canadian basketball landscape through development, commitment, leadership and vision, presented by Canada Basketball

James Norris Memorial Trophy—top defenceman, as selected by the Professional Hockey Writers' Association

Jeff Russel Memorial Trophy—CFL outstanding player in the East Division as selected by the Football Reporters of Canada

John Semmelink Memorial Award—Canada's most outstanding athlete in skiing and snowboarding, presented by the Canadian Snowsport Association

Lady Byng Memorial Trophy—NHL player who exhibited outstanding sportsmanship and gentlemanly conduct, combined with a high standard of playing ability, as selected by the Professional Hockey Writers' Association

Lester B. Pearson Award—Most outstanding NHL player in regular season, as selected by the members of the NHLPA

Lester Patrick Trophy—NHL player who has made a significant contribution to ice hockey in the United States, as selected by a committee of NHL officials

Lew Hayman Trophy—CFL's outstanding Canadian player in the East Division, as selected by the Football Reporters of Canada

Lionel Conacher Award—Canada's male athlete of the year, as selected by members of the Canadian Press

Lou Kaplan Trophy—WHA rookie of the year

Lou Marsh Memorial Trophy—Canada's top athlete, professional or amateur, as selected by a panel of journalists

M.A.C. Hermann Trophy—top U.S. male and female college soccer players, presented by the Missouri Athletic Club

Mike Kelly Medal—most outstanding player in lacrosse's Mann Cup, as selected by Canadian sports writers

Millar Trophy—presented to the winner of the CPGA championship

Norton H. Crow Award—outstanding male athlete of the year, presented by the True Sport Foundation

Order of Canada—recognizes a lifetime of outstanding achievement and merit in service to Canada or to humanity at large; there are 3 levels (in ranking order): Member, Officer, and Companion

Oscar Mathisen Award—international award for the outstanding speed skating performance of the season, as presented by the Oslo Skøiteklub (Oslo Skating Club)

Silver Slugger Award—MLB's best offensive player at each position in both American League and National League, as selected by MLB coaches and managers

Sovereign Award—Canada's outstanding jockey or man of the year, as presented by the Jockey Club of Canada

Thomas Keller Medal—outstanding international career in rowing, presented by the International Rowing Federation

Trico Goaltender Award—NHL goaltender with the best save percentage during the regular season. First presented in 1989; discontinued in 1992

Velma Springstead Award—outstanding female athlete of the year, presented by the True Sport Foundation

Vezina Trophy—NHL's top goaltender, as selected by 30 NHL general managers

William M. Jennings Trophy—NHL goaltender with the best goals-against record in the regular season

Wilma Rudolph Courage Award—female athlete who exhibits extraordinary courage in her athletic performance, overcomes adversity, makes significant contributions to sports, and serves as an inspiration and role model to those who face challenges, presented by the Women's Sports Foundation

Wilson and McCall Trophy—outstanding partners in a sporting event, presented by True Sport Foundation

World Curling Freytag Award—honours curlers for world-championship–level playing ability, sportsmanship, character, and the achievement of extraordinary distinction, presented by World Curling Federation

ATHLETES by Rank

47 Beckie Scott
46 George Chuvalo
45 Silken Laumann
44 Harry Jerome
43 Brian Orser
42 Kathleen Heddle
41 Sandy Hawley
40 Caroline Brunet
39 Marc Gagnon
38 Mark Messier
37 Patrick Roy
36 Tom Longboat
35 Justin Morneau
34 Bobby Hull
33 Victor Davis
32 Elvis Stojko
31 Martin Brodeur
30 Catriona Le May Doan
29 Lennox Lewis
28 Steve Podborski
27 Doug Harvey
26 Kurt Browning
25 Hayley Wickenheiser
24 Gaétan Boucher
23 Alex Baumann
22 Russ Jackson
21 Percy Williams
20 Marlene Stewart Streit

19 Bobbie Rosenfeld
18 Simon Whitfield
17 Chantal Petitclerc
16 Barbara Ann Scott
15 Mario Lemieux
14 Nancy Greene
13 Marnie McBean
12 Mike Weir
11 Maurice "Rocket" Richard
10 Clara Hughes
 9 Larry Walker
 8 Ferguson Jenkins
 7 Gordie Howe
 6 Donovan Bailey
 5 Lionel Conacher
 4 Cindy Klassen
 3 Steve Nash
 2 Bobby Orr
 1 Wayne Gretzky

SPECIAL HONOUR: Terry Fox

ALPHABETICAL Index of Athletes

Lewis, Lennox (29)
Longboat, Tom (36)
Longden, Johnny (59)
Magnussen, Karen (70)
Martin, Kevin (96)
McBean, Marnie (13)
McLarnin, Jimmy (80)
Messier, Mark (38)
Millar, Ian (53)
Morenz, Howie (65)
Morneau, Justin (35)
Nash, Steve (3)
Nattrass, Susan (95)
Nestor, Daniel (63)
Orr, Bobby (2)
Orser, Brian (43)
Pelletier, David (77)
Petitclerc, Chantal (17)
Podborski, Steve (28)
Post, Sandra (52)
Potvin, Denis (90)
Read, Ken (61)

Richard, Henri (89)
Richard, Maurice "Rocket" (11)
Robinson, Larry (100)
Rosenfeld, Bobbie (19)
Roy, Patrick (37)
Salé, Jamie (77)
Sawchuk, Terry (67)
Schmirler, Sandra (71)
Scott, Barbara Ann (16)
Scott, Beckie (47)
Shore, Eddie (78)
Sinclair, Christine (76)
Stewart Streit, Marlene (20)
Stojko, Elvis (32)
Tanner, Elaine (48)
Taylor, Fred "Cyclone" (74)
Tewksbury, Mark (94)
Turcotte, Ron (62)
van Koeverden, Adam (55)
Villeneuve, Gilles (75)
Villeneuve, Jacques (99)
Walker, Larry (9)
Weir, Mike (12)
Whitfield, Simon (18)
Wickenheiser, Hayley (25)
Williams, Percy (21)
Yzerman, Steve (54)

ATHLETES by Sport

MULTIPLE SPORTS
Jack Bionda (56)
Lionel Conacher (5)
Clara Hughes (11)
Ferguson Jenkins (8)
Cindy Klassen (4)
Bobbie Rosenfeld (19)

BASEBALL
Eric Gagné (57)
Ferguson Jenkins (8)
Justin Morneau (35)
Larry Walker (9)

BASKETBALL
Steve Nash (3)

BIATHLON
Myriam Bédard (60)

BOXING
Tommy Burns (73)
George Chuvalo (46)
Lionel Conacher (5)
Lennox Lewis (29)
Jimmy McLarnin (80)

CAR RACING
Gilles Villeneuve (75)
Jacques Villeneuve (99)

CROSS-COUNTRY SKIING
Beckie Scott (47)

CURLING
Kevin Martin (96)
Sandra Schmirler (71)

CYCLING
Steve Bauer (72)
Clara Hughes (10)

EQUESTRIAN
Ian Millar (53)

FIGURE SKATING
Kurt Browning (26)
Karen Magnussen (70)
Brian Orser (43)
David Pelletier (77)
Jamie Salé (77)
Barbara Ann Scott (16)
Elvis Stojko (32)

FOOTBALL
Lionel Conacher (5)
Tony Gabriel (82)
Russ Jackson (22)
Normie Kwong (86)

GOLF
George Knudson (51)
Sandra Post (52)
Marlene Stewart Streit (20)
Mike Weir (12)

HOCKEY
Syl Apps (87)
Jean Béliveau (49)
Jack Bionda (56)
Mike Bossy (93)
Ray Bourque (91)
Martin Brodeur (31)
Paul Coffey (64)
Lionel Conacher (5)
Phil Esposito (66)
Wayne Gretzky (1)
Doug Harvey (27)
Gordie Howe (7)
Bobby Hull (34)
Angela James (85)
Guy Lafleur (83)
Mario Lemieux (15)
Mark Messier (38)
Howie Morenz (65)
Bobby Orr (2)
Denis Potvin (90)
Henri Richard (89)
Maurice "Rocket" Richard (11)
Larry Robinson (100)
Bobbie Rosenfeld (19)
Patrick Roy (37)
Terry Sawchuk (67)
Eddie Shore (78)
Fred "Cyclone" Taylor (74)
Hayley Wickenheiser (25)
Steve Yzerman (54)

HORSE RACING
Sandy Hawley (41)
Johnny Longden (59)
Ron Turcotte (62)

KAYAKING
Caroline Brunet (40)
Adam van Koeverden (55)

LACROSSE
Jack Bionda (56)
Lionel Conacher (5)
Gary Gait (79)

MARATHON SWIMMING
Marilyn Bell (58)

ROWING
Ned Hanlan (84)
Kathleen Heddle (42)
Silken Laumann (45)
Marnie McBean (13)

SHOOTING
Susan Nattrass (95)

SKIING
Nancy Greene (14)
Anne Heggtveit (92)
Jennifer Heil (97)
Kathy Kreiner (69)
Steve Podborski (28)
Ken Read (61)

SOCCER
Charmaine Hooper (98)
Christine Sinclair (76)

SOFTBALL
Hayley Wickenheiser (25)

SPEED SKATING
Gaétan Boucher (24)
Marc Gagnon (39)
Clara Hughes (10)
Cindy Klassen (4)
Catriona Le May Doan (30)

SWIMMING
Alex Baumann (23)
Victor Davis (33)
Nancy Garapick (68)
Elaine Tanner (48)
Mark Tewksbury (94)

TENNIS
Daniel Nestor (63)

TRACK AND FIELD
Syl Apps (87)
Donovan Bailey (6)
Phil Edwards (81)
Harry Jerome (44)
Tom Longboat (36)
Bobbie Rosenfeld (19)
Percy Williams (21)

TRIATHALON
Simon Whitfield (18)

WHEELCHAIR RACING
Rick Hansen (50)
Chantal Petitclerc (17)

WRESTLING
Daniel Igali (88)

RESOURCES

The publications and websites of the following organizations were invaluable:
The Canadian Encyclopedia
The Canadian Press
CBC Sports
CTV Sports
The Historica-Dominion Institute
Jewish Women's Archive
Library and Archives Canada (Electronic Collection)
NBC Sports
TSN

Canada's Sports Hall of Fame and the Hockey Hall of Fame (and their affiliated site, Legends of Hockey) were particularly useful. Also helpful were the websites of each province's sports hall of fame, as well as these specific sport halls of fame:
Canadian Football Hall of Fame and Museum
Canadian Horse Racing Hall of Fame
Canadian Ski Hall of Fame
International Boxing Hall of Fame
International Swimming Hall of Fame
National Lacrosse League Hall of Fame

For fact-checking and confirming details, I am grateful to the websites of these sport organizations and associations:
Alpine Canada
Basketball Canada
BC Lacrosse Association
Canadian Association for the Advancement of Women and Sport and Physical Activity
Canadian Curling Association
Canadian Cycling Association
Canadian Equestrian Federation
Canadian Figure Skating Association
Canadian Football League

Canadian Ladies' Golf Association
Canadian Olympic Association
Canadian Paralympic Committee
Canadian Ski Association
Canadian Soccer Association
Edmonton Oilers Heritage
Hockey Canada
Major League Baseball
National Basketball Association
National Hockey League
Rowing Canada
Swimming Canada
Tennis Canada

These books were useful in my research:
Bisson, James. *One Hundred Greatest Canadian Sports Moments*. (Toronto: Wiley, 2008).
Dixon, Joan. *Trailblazing Sports Heroes*. (Canmore: Altitude, 2003).
Dryden, Steve. *Total Gretzky*. (Toronto: McClelland & Stewart, 2000).
Dublin, Anne. *Bobbie Rosenfeld: The Olympian Who Could Do Everything*. (Toronto: Second Story Press, 2004).
Etue, Elizabeth & Williams, Megan. *On The Edge: Women Making Hockey History*. (Toronto: Second Story Press, 1996).
Greene, Nancy, *Nancy Greene: An Autobiography*, (Learning Concepts, 1971).
Long, Wendy. *Celebrating Excellence: Canadian Women Athletes*. (Vancouver: Polestar, 1995).
MacSkimming, Roy. *Gordie: A Hockey Legend*. (Vancouver: Greystone Books, 2003).
Morrow, Don et al. *A Concise History of Sport in Canada*. (Toronto: Oxford University Press, 1998).
Wallechinsky, David. *The Complete Book of the Olympics: 2008 Edition*. (Aurum Press, 2008).
Zeman, Brenda. *To Run With Longboat*. (Edmonton, 1988).

The online and print versions of these newspapers and magazines provided background information and material:
Canadian Rowing
Chatelaine
The Globe and Mail
The Hockey News
Maclean's
New Mobility
The New York Times
The Province
The San Diego Union-Tribune
Sports Illustrated
The Toronto Star
The Vancouver Sun
United Athletes

These websites provided important information:
boxrec.com
blackhistorysociety.ca
cyberboxingzone.com
encyclopedia.stateuniversity.com
famouscanadians.net
formula1.com
heroines.ca
olympic.org
owha.on.ca
slam.canoe.ca
sports.jrank.org

I am grateful for the many detailed and well-maintained websites of individual athletes and teams.

PHOTOGRAPHY Credits

A special thanks to the following people whose hard work and efficiency made this excellent selection of images possible:

KATE BIRD from Pacific Newspaper Group

CRAIG CAMPBELL from the Hockey Hall of Fame

ANDREA GORDON from The Canadian Press Images

ARDEN HERBERT from Canada's Sports Hall of Fame

CRYSTAL SALAMON from Getty Images

These credits are listed alphabetically by the athletes' last name.

Syl Apps: Canada's Sports Hall of Fame

Donovan Bailey: (celebrating) AFP/Getty Images; (relay) Jeff Haynes/AFP/Getty Images

Steve Bauer: COC/The Canadian Press/ J. Merrithew

Alex Baumann: *The Province*

Myriam Bédard: The Canadian Press/ Ron Poling

Jean Béliveau: Harold Barkley Archives

Marilyn Bell: *Vancouver Sun*

Jack Bionda: *Vancouver Sun*

Mike Bossy: O-Pee-Chee/Hockey Hall of Fame

Gaétan Boucher: COC/The Canadian Press

Ray Bourque: Bruce Bennett/Bruce Bennett Studios/Getty Images

Martin Brodeur: Jim McIsaac/Getty Images

Kurt Browning: COC/The Canadian Press

Caroline Brunet: Maxim Marmur/AFP/ Getty Images

Tommy Burns: Canada's Sports Hall of Fame

George Chuvalo: *Vancouver Sun*/Ralph Bower

Paul Coffey: Steve Babineau/NHLI/Getty Images

Lionel Conacher: (hockey) Hockey Hall of Fame; (football and boxing) Canada's Sports Hall of Fame

Victor Davis: COC/The Canadian Press/Cromby McNeil

Phil Edwards: Canada's Sports Hall of Fame

Phil Esposito: Tony Triolo/Sports Illustrated/Getty Images

Terry Fox: (portrait) The Canadian Press/Chuck Stoody; (Order of Canada): *Vancouver Sun*/Glenn Baglo; (running) The Canadian Press

Tony Gabriel: The Canadian Press/ Arne Glassbourg

Eric Gagné: The Canadian Press/ Jeff Lewis

Marc Gagnon: Donald Miralle/ Getty Images

Gary Gait: The Canadian Press/ Geoff Robins

Nancy Garapick: *The Province*/John Denniston

Nancy Greene: Canada's Sports Hall of Fame

Wayne Gretzky: (young Oiler) *The Province*/Rick Loughran; (from above) The Canadian Press/Dave Buston; (Stanley Cup) The Canadian Press/Mike Ridewood; (Los Angeles) The Canadian Press/Michael Tweed; (New York) Jim McIsaac/Bruce Bennett Studios/Getty Images; (Team Canada) COC/The Canadian Press/ F. Scott Grant

Ned Hanlan: Canada's Sports Hall of Fame

Rick Hansen: *Vancouver Sun*/Ian Lindsay

Doug Harvey: Imperial Oil—Turofsky/ Hockey Hall of Fame

Sandy Hawley: *Vancouver Sun*/Ken Oakes

Kathleen Heddle: COC/The Canadian Press/Mike Ridewood

Anne Heggtveit: Canada's Sports Hall of Fame

Jennifer Heil: The Canadian Press/ Lee Jin-man

Charmaine Hooper: *The Province*/ Arlen Redekop

Gordie Howe: (Detroit) Harold Barkley Archives; (Hartford): The Canadian Press/Doug Ball

Clara Hughes: (cycling) The Canadian Press/Frank Gunn; (with flag) *The Province*/Gerry Kahrmann; (skating) *Vancouver Sun*/Ian Lindsay

Bobby Hull: Harold Barkley Archives

Daniel Igali: COC/The Canadian Press

Russ Jackson: *Vancouver Sun*

Angela James: Matthew Manor/Hockey Hall of Fame

Ferguson Jenkins: (young) Louis Requena/MLB Photos/Getty Images; (pitching) Focus on Sport/Getty Images

Harry Jerome: *The Province*/Bill Cunningham

Cindy Klassen: (with medals) The Canadian Press/Paul Chiasson; (skating) The Canadian Press/ Jeff McIntosh

George Knudson: Canada's Sports Hall of Fame

Kathy Kreiner: COC/The Canadian Press

Normie Kwong: *Vancouver Sun*

Guy Lafleur: Denis Brodeur/NHLI/ Getty Images

Silken Laumann: Mike Powell/Getty Images

Catriona Le May Doan: *Toronto Star*/ The Canadian Press/Richard Lautens

Mario Lemieux: David Maxwell/AFP/ Getty Images

Lennox Lewis: COC/The Canadian Press/S. Grant

132

CONTRIBUTORS

The Canadian
Sport Advisory Council:

ROBIN BROWN is an award-winning broadcaster with CBC Radio. She has covered professional and amateur sports for 20 years, including seven Olympic Games.

CAM COLE has been writing a daily sports column for the last 21 years, currently with the *Vancouver Sun* and previously as the principal sports columnist at the *National Post* and at the *Edmonton Journal*.

MARY JOLLIMORE spent 25 years as a sports journalist working for Reuters, TIME magazine, the CBC, and as a columnist at *The Globe and Mail*. She now teaches journalism at Loyalist College in Ontario.

Freelance writer **WENDY LONG** is an Advisory Board Member at Canada's Sports Hall of Fame. For more than 20 years, she was a sports reporter with the *Vancouver Sun*, covering six Olympic Games and other major international sporting events.

GARY MASON is a national columnist with *The Globe and Mail*. A two-time Jack Webster Award recipient, Mason covered politics and sports for the *Vancouver Sun* for almost 20 years.

MARY ORMSBY is Associate Sports Editor with the *Toronto Star*, and appears regularly on the sports talk radio show *Prime Time Sports*. She is a former member of Canada's junior and senior volleyball teams.

Veteran hockey broadcaster **JIM ROBSON** was "The Voice of the Canucks" for nearly three decades. He covered hockey and other sports for a variety of television and radio networks.

JIM TAYLOR has written more than 7,500 sports columns and 13 books. His passionate sports writing has earned him membership in the CFL and BC Sports Halls of Fame and a lifetime achievement award from Sports Media Canada.

ED WILLES is a senior sports writer with *The Province* in Vancouver. He has covered sports from major centres across the country, including Regina, Winnipeg, and Montreal.

. . .

MAGGIE MOONEY is a writer, community worker, and sports fan. She is co-author of *Nobel's Women of Peace*, and lives on Gabriola Island, British Columbia.